THE DEVOURING FUNGUS

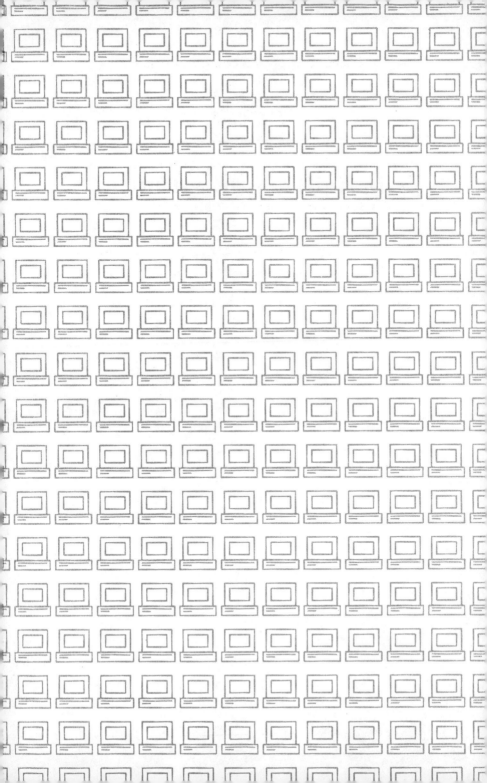

THE DEVOURING FUNGUS

TALES OF THE COMPUTER AGE

KARLA JENNINGS

W. W. NORTON & COMPANY
NEW YORK   LONDON

Illustration credits:
Chapter 1: Advertisement from *Popular Science,* October 1946. Photograph courtesy Charles Babbage Institute, University of Minnesota. Chapters 2, 6, 7, 8: Cartoons by Richard Tennant. Permission by artist. Chapter 3: Cartoon by G. B. Trudeau. *Doonesbury* copyright 1989 G. B. Trudeau. Reprinted with permission of Universal Press Syndicate. All rights reserved. Chapter 4: Cartoons by Dick Locher and Max Collins. Reprinted by permission: Tribune Media Services. Chapter 5: Cartoon by Sidney Harris. Permission by artist. Chapter 9: Cartoon by Mike Peters. Permission by United Media. Chapter 10: Cartoon by McKee. Reproduced by permission of *Punch.*

The text of this book is composed in Avanta,
with the display set in Eterna.
Composition and manufacturing by the Haddon Craftsmen, Inc.
Book design by Debbie Glasserman.

Library of Congress Cataloging-in-Publication Data

Jennings, Karla.
The devouring fungus: tales of the computer age / by Karla Jennings.
p. cm.
1. Computers and civilization. I. Title.
QA76.9.C66J46 1990
303.48′34—dc20   90–31461

ISBN 0-393-02897-6
ISBN 0-393-30732-8 PBK.

W. W. Norton & Company, Inc.
500 Fifth Avenue, New York, N.Y. 10110

W. W. Norton & Company, Ltd.
10 Coptic Street, London WC1A 1PU

2 3 4 5 6 7 8 9 0

For Warner and Stella Jennings
who programmed me with love and understanding
and made me strong

CONTENTS

CONTENTS

INTRODUCTION

Ants farm, chimps make tools, and even a dachshund can wear designer sweaters, but only one species tells lies—ah, legends. Man is the animal that tells stories. You won't see a marmot hanging out in bars swapping tall tales, unless it's an unusual marmot, but people do it as a matter of course, as compelled to turn their lives into legend as they are to eat and sleep.

Legend-weaving continues even though we're long past the age of miracles. No matter how logical we like to think we are, mystical tales burst through our rationality to feed our hunger for stories. We laugh at the idea that stars control our destinies, but we read horoscopes.

A lot of people might reasonably wonder whether, despite this, legends can grow in the computer culture's hard, dry soil. Those of us without any particular mathematical gift tend to dismiss computers as boring and computer professionals as equally dull. I think some of that scorn comes from intimidation. For those of us who banged our heads on the brick wall of incomprehension over negative numbers until we realized that a negative number is just like owing the lunch lady a nickel, classmates who porpoised through mathematical seas with casual ease were daunting, even creepy. It wouldn't be surprising if, in prehistoric times, such people were the tribe's medicine women and shamans, with their unearthly instinct for the constellations. In a later age, they would have been the astrologers, as well as some of the witches burned at the stake. Take this description of a math prodigy who, if he'd shown his stuff a few centuries earlier instead of in 1846, would have been called the devil's child. Even the parson who tested his ability describes him as acting like one possessed:

> Then said I, "Multiply, in your head, 365, 365, 365, 365, 365 by 365, 365, 365, 365, 365, 365!"
> He flew round the room like a top, pulled his pantaloons over the top of his boots, bit his hand, rolled his eyes in their sockets, sometimes smiling and talking, and then seeming to be in agony, until, in not more than one minute, said he, "133,491,850,208,566,925,016,658,299,941,583,225!"
> The boy's father, Rev. C. N. Smith, and myself, had each a pencil and slate to take down the answer, and he gave it to us in periods of three figures each, as fast as it was possible for us to write them. And what was still more wonderful, he began to multiply at the left hand, and to bring out the answer from left to right, giving first "133, 491," &c. Here, confounded above measure, I gave up the examination. The boy looked pale, and said he was tired. He said it was the largest sum he had ever done!

The boy, Truman Safford, become an astronomer at the University of Chicago.

The computer culture's intimidating power, as well as the pride its adherents take in being literal and exact, could make even the most optimistic of us skeptical about the possibility of its having legends. I doubted it myself while starting research by going to the University of California at Berkeley to interview computer science students. Toddling about Evans Hall, I wandered into a room where the software maven Richard Stallman was working. Students said the university hired him at an ungodly salary to devise a new compiler; he was hacking away at a terminal, his clothing bedraggled, his forehead tendriled with unwashed hair, looking pretty much like any grad student during finals week. I asked if he knew any computer fables, and he turned, looked at me with watchful eyes, and said, "I'm afraid not. I have trouble remembering what isn't real." Though he did offer to tell me true stories later, it wasn't exactly a slam-bang beginning for the book.

However, over time I discovered that computer professionals love a good tale as much as anyone. Quite a few have no problem letting fancy drown out credibility, such as a landlady I once had who was a software consultant for major financial institutions. She possessed the calculating rapaciousness of most landladies whose condition is aggravated by a close professional relationship with bankers. She was also an expert in past lives, auras, natal charts, and astrology. One morning when I was just stepping out on my way to work, she burst from her bedroom screaming, "The moon is in Aquarius and, God, am I horny!" If a software computer consultant believes her gonads are ruled by the moon, then none of us is safe.

Other computer people were careful to tell true events as accurately as possible, taking a keener pleasure in the stories because of their added impact for being real. Real or false, many of the stories have an imaginative force that implies they flow from the same mystical river of creativity running through other sciences as well as the arts. As the mythologist Joseph Campbell put it in voluptuous scholarly prose: "Religions, philosophies, arts, the social forms of primitive and historic man, prime discoveries in science and technology, the very dreams that blister sleep, boil up from the basic, magic ring of myth."

Examples of how mystical experiences lead to scientific breakthroughs are easy to find. Take Friedrich Kekule von

Stradonitz, a nineteenth-century German chemist confounded by the formula for benzene. No one could figure out how the carbon atoms of this common compound stuck together. He scribbled through miles of formulas, gave up, and lay back exhausted by the fire, staring with half-closed eyes at the flames. Inside the fire he imagined a snake rolling around like a hoop, its tail in its mouth.

His eyes snapped open. Of course! the carbon atoms formed a ring! His discovery of the benzene ring helped form the basis for modern organic chemistry, yet the symbol of the rolling snake with its tail in its mouth springs from many ancient cultures, an image of life constantly consuming and renewing itself.

Another researcher, an electrical engineer working on forerunners of modern computers, dreamed a dream during the bloody spring of 1940 that grew into one of the first uses of the computer as a weapon against the Third Reich. That spring, Hitler's troops roared across Holland, Belgium, and France, while retreating British troops massed at Dunkirk, knowing they would be slaughtered, and desperate because England's naval fleet didn't have enough ships to evacuate them.

D. B. Parkinson was the engineer. He was working at Bell Labs in the United States on an electronic device called an automatic level recorder. It had a potentiometer—a device to measure voltage differences—that guided a recording pen. It was an intriguing machine, but no one knew what to do with it.

Helplessly pinned in at Dunkirk, the British could do little but die under heavy Stuka bombardment. American newspapers described their dilemma.

"It preyed on everyone's mind—mine included," recalled Parkinson.

I had been working on the level recorder for several weeks when one night I had this most vivid and peculiar dream.

I found myself in a gun pit or revetment with an anti-aircraft gun crew. I don't know how I got there—I was just there. The men were Dutch or Belgian by their uniforms—the helmets were neither German, French, nor English. There was [an anti-aircraft] gun there. . . . It was firing occasionally, and the impressive thing was that *every shot brought down an airplane!* After three or four shots one of the men in the crew smiled at me and beckoned me to come closer to the gun. When I drew near he pointed to the exposed end of the left trunnion. Mounted there was the control potentiometer of my level recorder! There was no mistaking it—it was the identical item.

The whole scene then faded out, and some time later I woke up, still retaining a remarkably clear memory of the details. It didn't take long to make the necessary translation—if the potentiometer could control the high-speed motion of a recording pen with great accuracy, why couldn't a suitably engineered device do the same thing for an anti-aircraft gun!

His dream led to anti-aircraft gun directors using primitive computers to interpret radar data to pinpoint targets. It was part of the technological upheaval of World War II, the beginning of the age in which electronics fed the power of mass destruction and retaliation. For the first time, telephone systems and electromechanical computers tightened weapons' deadly accuracy.

The legends dreamed up by the computer culture often have a surrealistic aura, where the rough world of rotten bananas and plunging boulders fuses with the ethereal one of abstract precision. An example is a story whose very sketchiness lures the reader to speculate:

A railroad company hired a computer firm in the early 'sixties to keep track of freight cars and inventory. During the course of adding each freight car to the computer tally, railroad people rummaging around freight yards in Los Angeles found a boxcar filled with brand new, ten-year-old automobiles. They also discovered a carload of hides that had been shuttling back and forth between Los Angeles and Kansas City for years, during which time the hides had gotten pretty ripe.

It's tempting to imagine what kind of cars they were. Were they new Edsels, headlights smashed from banging into each other through a thousand rattles and rolls? Or red Sunbirds, their upholstery cracked by smoldering for ten summers in an airless metal box, the glue holding up their rearview mirrors baking off in the constant blast until one by one each mirror crashes onto its dashboard? And those ripe hides! They could have been the last shipment of slaughtered buffalo skins from the Old West, a bloody treasure rotting and sliding endlessly back and forth in pointless travels, never reaching the parlors of people who now are as dead as those buffalo.

The computer surprises us by pulling out lost craziness in our world, and offers more craziness of its own. If a computerized dating service can help you choose the perfect mate, maybe it *will* select your ex-wife. If it knows everything in the world, maybe it *will* declare itself God, or tell you the man you think is your father really isn't, or seduce you into baring your soul to it more quickly than to any human. Computer tales are also strange because computers live not in our material world but in a mathematical universe, an Alice in Wonderland realm where anything is possible.

The rational and the fantastic hold an uneasy dual reign in computer stories because they reflect the uneasy duality in their makers. What better creation for spinning legends than one which closely mimics its creator, giving us a reflection so near to human, but different?

Like us, the computer is a fusion of good and evil. It can

make your life more efficient, and more cold. It helps dictators cast electronic nets over the common man's most vulnerable secrets and ruthlessly pull them in, but it helps commoners depose murderous tyrants by beaming their bloodthirstiness to the world and making us all witnesses. It educates kids in our schools, but makes it harder for the uneducated to find menial jobs, which are being computerized out of existence. Those who don't understand computers are becoming a new under-class, cut off from the information that gives others an advan-tage, and from the skills for survival in the marketplace. At the same time, computers might turn back the tide of this postliter-ate age by renewing the need for coherent, organized speech. All the English majors afraid they'll be flipping burgers for a living needn't worry: robots will steal the burger-flipping jobs from you, but computers will increase the demand for people who know how to turn computerese into plain English, a talent lacking in those drowning in CompuSpeak.

The stories show our irresistible habit of anthropomorphiz-ing the computer, a habit we indulge in with just about any machine, something advertisers exploit when they turn dish-washers into talking cubes and car rides into sexual intercourse. The limits of our imagination might be one reason we an-thropomorphize things: we're incapable of understanding an exploding star or a VCR except in how it relates to us and is like us. From God to the devil to the big wide world, we look out and see ourselves. Perhaps if we saw the world through cat's eyes, we'd be able to understand it only insofar as it relates to cats—squirrels, fish, mice, and rats would make us ache with desire, humans would be spindly clowns that feed us, and the world's most useless beast would be the dog.

Because they're so much like us in the first place, we seem to find it unusually easy to turn computers into alter egos. A Hous-tonian said in an interview, "The computer is just sort of an extension of my brain and something that I have, from the beginning, dealt with as familiarly and effortlessly as I deal with my own brain."

Fascination with the computer's endlessly unfolding universe can become an obsession, a rapture of the deep, a form of reflected self-love that can turn the computer into a soul mate. Another Houstonian recalled, "When I first got introduced to the computer, it was really in very many ways like falling in love or like having a real strong infatuation. And I would think about my computer at night and didn't want to be away from my computer. I didn't want to go teach my classes, because I had to leave my computer. It's just like when I was in college and I met my wife, met the girl that became my wife. We would want to be together all the time during that first initial falling-in-love phase."

The computer's intimacy with our psyches makes for revealing stories. What do the tales reveal about the community that created them?

They show a self-aware, self-conscious community that mistrusts outsiders, especially those in authority who hire and fire computer experts and hold the purse strings for making technological miracles, but who don't share the purist's love for the machine. The community treasures the iconoclast, the outcast, and freedom, and despises authority and bureaucracy.

In some tales, the computer is the programmer's ally, exposing outsiders as pea brains who can't tell a microchip from a potato chip. Others show delight in bizarre tricks, such as making computer parts walk out of their cabinets. Stories that reverse the roles of master and servant give voice to the anxiety many people feel toward computers. Electronic replicas of folklore characters such as the Trickster, the Fool, and the Wise One spring up throughout the book, though sometimes they are in disguise: a Wise One can just as easily be a machine as a person.

About four hundred of the approximately five hundred anecdotes, jokes, terms, koans, parables, graphics, and visions of mass hysteria I collected made the final cut for this book. I haven't tracked down each story from its teller to its original source to see which "true" stories are legend and which legends spring from fact. Those interested in such matters can begin with the source guide at the back of the book and take it from there. Instead, I've tried to arrange and tell the tales in the best storytelling manner possible, mixing them into a stew spiced with elaboration. If you don't find it tasty, you're welcome to return to the macaroni and cheese of bare life.

Whatever you feel about the computer, you have to admit that it's there, it's not going to go away, and it's going to get bigger. The changes even in the last fifteen years are immense. I remember as a college freshman buying my first calculator, something called a Slide Rule II, which was about the size of a two-pound package of cheddar cheese. I put it in its carrying case and wore it on my belt like a six-shooter. It cost $75 (this was in 1974, when $75 meant something), but it was worth it because it could add, subtract, multiply, and divide. Today, a calculator with twice the functions of that bulky dinosaur might be an eighth its size and a tenth its cost. The computer defies clichés for success: bigger isn't better; smaller is better. To get more, you don't have to pay more; just wait for next year's cheaper, faster, more powerful model.

Some of this book's stories will already sound quaint to computer people, whose art flickers through transformations like Proteus. Vaccum tubes (or "valves" as the British call them) begat transistors, transistors begat integrated circuits, integrated circuits begat S-seeds and optical computers, which use laser beams instead of wire and promise to make fifth-generation technology look as dated as Victorian steam engines someday. It's possible that between the time you enter this book and the time you exit it, another discovery will be born that in its relentless maturity will overthrow much of our electronic empire.

Constant revolution demands that those following computer technology continue learning long after most people fall into comfortable ruts. They must stay used to confronting the new, because stagnancy in the computer industry means quick death. The widening spiral of computer innovation and social permeation is dizzying, especially when you consider that the fusion of biology and computers in artificial intelligence and in medicine will affect us on an increasingly intimate level. Who knows but that forty years from now, people said to have computers in their blood really *will* have computers in their blood, helping restore ruined kidneys, livers, lungs, and portions of the brain, as today's computerized pacemakers replace pacemaking cells destroyed by heart disease. Calling computers as ubiquitous as television, hair mousse, or even fungus may be underestimating the computer's prevalence.

Speaking of which, this book is titled *The Devouring Fungus* because it contains a story about a somewhat fungal computer bug that devours all in its path and, more important, because the computer's social infiltration is like that fungus, spreading everywhere. Computers feed on ignorance, the data explosion, the proliferation of new technology demanding exactitude, the rage for computer games, and the desire for convenience and ease, growing larger with each bite. You might find the presence of such a hungry pet unnerving, and accuse the computer of wanting to feed on *you,* but the computer isn't to blame for reflecting your fears. After all, it only mirrors our dreams, even if it is the queen of tools by which we change the world.

ACKNOWLEDGMENTS

Writing a book like this is like holding a yard sale in reverse; hundreds of people come to cover your empty tables with trinkets, knickknacks, second-hand tales, sometimes a jewel or fine watch. By the day's end, the tables creak under mountains of treasure and the people have disappeared. You've thanked some, but many you cannot thank, because they were anonymous or you've forgotten their names. Since I've held this reverse yard sale for three years, and have moved twice during that time, some names were lost in time and space. If yours is one of them, please don't mistake my forgetfulness for ingratitude.

A few names survived lost notes and memory's decay. One is Harry Gammerdinger, who braved the hackers' lairs of MIT to write his senior thesis on computer folklore, the zygote that grew into this book. Some of its stories are in these pages, as well as other tales Harry contributed. The second person responsible for this fine mess is Mary Cunnane of W. W. Norton, who despite my optimistic ignorance about what was involved in tackling such an odd project took me on. Dan

Conaway was her partner in pain. Together they battled through early drafts, spilling gallons of their own red ink so that a better story would see the light of dawn. Your country will never forget you, or at least I won't.

Then there's Mary L. Gray-Baker of Berkeley, California, who spent hours digging through the University of California at Berkeley folklore archives, searching for computer tales. And there's my cybernetic savior, Vernard C. Martin, who parted the waters of technology so that I could send and receive e-mail messages, and whose patience withstood my constant whine of "Why won't this damn machine work?" Rich Tennant showed special generosity in giving permission to use his cartoons, and people like Danny Sharpe of West Georgia College, Hal Webre of Cantonment, Florida, Russ Kepler of Albuquerque, New Mexico, and Neal Coulter of Florida Atlantic University mailed and told me great tales, and led me to more storytellers. There's also Henry Cate III (tell Henry IV to leave Wales alone!), who e-mailed me pounds of legends and jokes, outdoing even Bill Bulko of the University of Texas, who also took the time to gather and send me stories. J. A. N. Lee, editor in chief of the *Annals of the History of Computing,* bushwhacked me at a computer conference to turn me on to his journal, which was a tremendous resource, and read the history chapter for accuracy. *SIGSOFT Software Engineering Notes* was another great resource; it is edited by Peter G. Neumann, whose pernicious proclivity for puns is redeemed by his keen eye for weird tales. The software entrepeneur Steve Stawarz scrutinized some of the early chapters, and Ken Rimey kindly mailed me the netwire jargon dictionary. Dozens of people whom I personally interviewed showed the best side of the computer culture's personality; they were friendly, helpful, and interested.

Lastly, I must thank the man of numbers, who often had

more confidence in me than I did in myself. Without the man of numbers, I would not be a woman of letters.

Karla Jennings
May 20, 1990
Decatur, Georgia

THE DEVOURING FUNGUS

HOW MUCH IS $\sqrt[3]{2589^{16}}$?

The Army's ENIAC can give you the answer in a fraction of a second!

Think that's a stumper? You should see *some* of the ENIAC's problems! Brain twisters that if put to paper would run off this page and feet beyond . . . addition, subtraction, multiplication, division — square root, cube root, any root. Solved by an incredibly complex system of circuits operating 18,000 electronic tubes and tipping the scales at 30 tons!

The ENIAC is symbolic of many amazing Army devices with a brilliant future for you! The new Regular Army needs men with aptitude for scientific work, and as one of the first trained in the post-war era, you stand to get in on the ground floor of important jobs

YOUR REGULAR ARMY SERVES THE NATION AND MANKIND IN WAR AND PEACE

which have never before existed. You'll find that an Army career pays off.

The most attractive fields are filling quickly. Get into the swim while the getting's good! 1½, 2 and 3 year enlistments are open in the Regular Army to ambitious young men 18 to 34 (17 with parents' consent) who are otherwise qualified. If you enlist for 3 years, you may choose your own branch of the service, of those still open. Get full details at your nearest Army Recruiting Station.

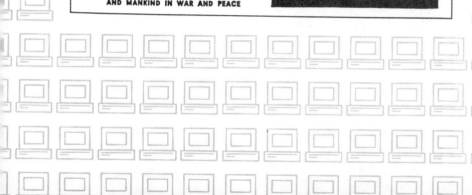

A GOOD JOB FOR YOU

U. S. Army

CHOOSE THIS
FINE PROFESSION NOW!

1

A KEEN MACHINE:
THE EVOLUTION OF
THE COMPUTER REVOLUTION

When CBS broadcast the Dwight Eisenhower/Adlai Stevenson III presidential election in 1952, it had a gimmick—
an enormous machine called a "computer" or "UNIVAC"
would predict the winner. A television reporter called the
UNIVAC a "he" and declared, pointing to its computer-
controlled typewriter, "When he wants to say something,
the keys move with no hands touching them! . . . Can you
say something, UNIVAC, do you have anything to say to
the television audience?" When it didn't respond, he noted,
"You're a very impolite machine."

But later UNIVAC did have something to say, something
that made even Walter Cronkite's coiffure stand on end.
Analyzing three percent of the returns, it predicted Eisenhower winning by a landslide. But polls showed a close race,
and Eisenhower was Republican, while the Democratic
South hadn't even been counted yet! So, officials from Remington Rand, UNIVAC's manufacturer, tampered with the
data to make UNIVAC broadcast a close race. But when
more returns showed Eisenhower burying Stevenson, the
president of Remington Rand appeared on the air to explain

to viewers that they'd fudged the data because they couldn't
believe their own computer. It was the television debut of
the computer age.

The computer's past is like a drunkard's dance: two steps
forward, one step back, a stagger to the left, a lurch to the right.
It's amazing that tipsy soft shoe added up to anything, let alone
the powerful and precise beast that is the computer. Yet it did,
despite failure and tragedy.

Take Wilhelm Schickard, a German craftsman and linguistics genius in the 1600s. During an age when witches were still
burned at the stake, he built a "calculating clock" that could
add and subtract. Unfortunately, his clock had bad timing. Fire
destroyed the prototype; then the Thirty Years' War erupted.
Before it ended, Schickard died of plague and his family died as
well, and the clock disappeared. Only centuries later did someone discover descriptions of Schickard's clock, which would
have been revolutionary if history hadn't so thoroughly erased
the clock maker.

Then there was Blaise Pascal of France, who twenty years
after Schickard's clock built a mechanical calculator to help his
tax collector father figure debts. Pascal was nineteen at the
time, already an outstanding mathematician. He cut short his
inventing by taking vows at a Jansenist community, spending
the rest of his life writing tirades against Jesuits and atheists.

The most poignant computer story is that of the collaboration between Charles Babbage (1791–1871) and Ada Byron
(1815–1852). Both were tempestuous mavericks, and both paid
the price for being different in a society that adored convention—Victorian England.

Babbage came from a wealthy banking family. He was an
eccentric who as a boy dabbled in black magic and as a man
bore such hatred for street musicians that they came from miles
around to mock him by playing beneath his window. His math-

ematical papers earned him election to the Royal Society, but he also wrote on odd topics such as scams used by London beggars. He was hot tempered, determined, and arrogant, had a knack for alienating others, and lacked a sense of economy despite his banking background. When the Royal Treasury gave him £1,500 to build a mechanical computer, he took what was possibly the country's first science grant and turned it into its first research budget overrun, going broke before the machine was done. He grew enraged when the government refused to give him more money to finish his computer, called the Difference Engine. Babbage might have wasted his life in spats with His Majesty's government if Ada Byron hadn't appeared. She became his goddess of the machine, his "enchantress of numbers." She was only seventeen.

Ada Byron was the sole legitimate child of the poet Lord Byron. She rarely saw her father, because her mother, disgusted by Byron's affair with his own half-sister, forbade him to visit. As a girl, Ada liked to build miniature ships and had a passion for mathematics. She was headstrong and independent, always fighting her dictatorial mother. She first met Babbage at a gathering at his estate, where he showed off his half-built Difference Engine.

"While other visitors gazed at the working of this beautiful instrument with the sort of expression, and I dare say the sort of feeling, that some savages are said to have shown on first seeing a looking glass . . . Miss Byron, young as she was, understood its working, and saw the great beauty of the invention," another guest later wrote.

The two wild spirits immediately found kinship, forming one of history's oddest couples: the curmudgeon widower and the beautiful daughter of a famous artist. Ada married and became Lady Lovelace, but craved the excitement that isn't found within the bonds of holy matrimony. She got it, too. She took her pleasure in liquor, cocaine, men—she had at least one affair—and the racetrack, twice pawning family jewels to pay gambling debts.

When Babbage started on a better computer, the Analytical Engine—which like today's computers had a memory and a central processing unit—Ada Lovelace wrote the best surviving description of how it worked. When he invented a way to program the Engine with punched cards, she used them to design the world's first computer program (the Pentagon honored her memory years later when it named its new program language ADA).

Babbage hadn't finished his first Analytical Engine before he hit on an idea for a better one. He soon had a worldwide reputation as a gifted mathematician and inventor. He was on the verge of creating the first useful, widely known calculator to tremendously shorten the time needed to solve complicated equations, with enormous implications for science, industry, and finance.

But he failed. And he failed by his own hand.

The first computer engineer fell victim to the first computer malady: the endless compulsion for perfection, an obsession choking out any interest in a creation's practical use or the importance of finishing a job. Victims of what could be called Babbage disease get too caught up in a project's intricacies to finish it, spending endless hours tinkering with details. They abandon half-finished projects for the seductive dreams of bigger challenges.

"One of the sad memories of my life is a visit to the celebrated mathematician and inventor, Mr. Babbage," recalled an acquaintance, Lord Moulton.

He was far advanced in age, but his mind was still as vigorous as ever. He took me through his workrooms. In the first room I saw the parts of the original Calculating Machine, which had been shown in an incomplete state many years before and had even been put to some use. I asked him about its present form.

"I have not finished it because in working at it I came on the idea of my Analytical Machine, which would do all that it was capable of doing and much more," [said Babbage]. "So I turned my attention to the Analytical Machine."

After a few minutes' talk we went into the next workroom, where he showed and explained to me the working of the elements of the Analytical Machine. I asked if I could see it.

"I have never completed it," he said, "because I hit upon an idea of doing the same thing by a different and far more effective method, and this rendered it useless to proceed on the old lines."

Then we went into the third room. There lay scattered bits of mechanism, but I saw no trace of any working machine.

Very cautiously I approached the subject, and received the dreaded answer, "It is not constructed yet, but I am working at it, and it will take less time to construct it altogether than it would have taken to complete the Analytical Machine from the stage in which I left it."

I took leave of the old man with a heavy heart.

Lady Lovelace developed cancer. Unable to control her wild child when Ada was healthy, her mother now dominated her with a vengeance. She withheld morphine despite her daughter's agony and prevented Babbage from visiting, though Ada wanted to make him her executor. Ada died at age thirty-six, after months of pain.

Alone in his dotage, Babbage wasted most of his personal fortune in his doomed pursuit of the perfect engine. A friend wrote after visiting the aged maverick that his drawing room "looked dreary in the extreme; the furniture had the stiff primness of age. . . . The place was dimly lighted by four candles, the grate yawned black and fireless, for it was not yet winter." When Babbage died, Lord Moulton wrote that "the verdict of a jury of kind and sympathetic scientific men who were deputed to pronounce upon what he had left behind him, either in papers or mechanism, was that everything was too incomplete to be capable of being put to any useful purpose."

The gentlemanly research pace Babbage enjoyed vanished with his century. Breakthroughs such as Henry Ford's assembly line and catastrophes such as World War I whipped technology into a race fueled by the hothouse economics of the Roaring Twenties. The computer no longer depended on the interest of wealthy eccentrics to stay alive. It now had a life of its own.

Researchers on three continents strained to make a machine to master the equations governing the world, equations grown out of control. Industrialists, engineers, scientists, and statisticians spent months grinding out formulas, then grinding through them again. In the United States, the population was multiplying faster than humans could count. The U.S. census took years to tabulate; by the time the 1880 census data were processed, it was almost time for the 1890 census.

Herman Hollerith of Manhattan stepped in to save the eyesight of hundreds of exhausted census tabulators. He developed punch-card-controlled computing machines that tabulated the 1890 U.S. census in a few months. Businesses ordered slews of Hollerith machines, and he grew rich. He sold out to an entrepreneur who founded the Computing-Tabulating-Recording Company, or CTR. A salesman named Thomas Watson started working for CTR in 1914 and rose to the post of company president, transforming CTR into an international corporation with thousands of employees. Computer-Tabulating-Recording Company was too old-fashioned a name for such a behemoth, so the company changed it to International Business Machines (IBM).

Ideas and technology now flew together. Researchers built weird hybrids of wires and gears, electronics and mechanics, creatures bridging the gulf between Babbage's quaint engines and more-agile, powerful electronic beasts. Each machine used one of two figuring methods inherited from either the abacus or the slide rule.

The abacus uses digital computing: a bead represents a discrete unit, the way a finger does when we count to ten. Early digital computers used vacuum tubes to symbolize discrete units as well. A tube that was off could mean "zero," while a tube that was on could mean "one." Each tube represented a different number, and scores of blinking vacuum tubes calculated equations.

The slide rule uses analog computing; instead of using discrete units, analog computing measures lengths to represent the answer. The slide rule measured lengths along a wooden slipstick. An analog computer measured the length or intensity of electrical impulses, storing the charge in vacuum tubes.

MIT's Vannevar Bush started building an analog computing machine in 1930 with wheels and shafts. It took days to program and made many errors, but Bush finished it before building a better machine with 2,000 vacuum tubes that programmed with paper tape. Bush's analyzer weighed a hundred tons. It had 150 motors, about two hundred miles of wire, and thousands of electromechanical relays, newfangled devices used in telecommunications to switch signals on and off. Programmers wired the relays into plugboards, reprogramming by replugging wires in different patterns.

Intrigued by such strange designs, a Harvard physics student named Howard Aiken drew up plans for a supercalculator, but a lab technician told him not to waste his time building junk when the lab already had a calculator no one used. Aiken demanded to see it, and the technician led him to an attic where a model of part of Babbage's Difference Engine gleamed beneath the dust.

Aiken was transfixed. He'd never heard of Babbage but felt

the long-dead Englishman's spirit. He grabbed up everything he could read on him and grew fond of saying, "If Babbage had lived 75 years later, I would have been out of a job." Though Babbage's engine was of no practical use, his struggle inspired Aiken to keep going despite the apathy of others.

Aiken designed his "Proposed Automatic Calculating Machine" in 1937, but spent two years peddling it to indifferent companies. A manager at the Monroe Calculating Machine Company advised him to contact IBM.

"If Monroe had decided the pay the bill, this thing would have been made out of mechanical parts," said Aiken years later. "If RCA had been interested, it might have been electronic. And it was made out of tabulating machine parts because IBM was willing to pay the bill." Thus began the Mark I computer.

By then, the military had a deadly need for computers. Military arsenals, their power refined in the human testing fields of World War I, demanded greater precision in ballistics and anti-aircraft logistics. And the Nazis were marching.

Despite Hitler's relentless creep toward catastrophe, most people couldn't believe they might be destroyed in another nightmare when bodies from the War to End All Wars were still fresh in their graves. Hitler fed that illusion, even giving IBM's Thomas Watson the Order of Merit of the German Eagle with Star, assuring him, "There is to be no war." Three years later, a contemptuous Watson returned the medal. Hitler retaliated by forbidding him to set foot in Germany.

Back in England, while Winston Churchill fumed in political exile and Neville Chamberlain extolled Hitler's love of peace, a young man slept through his math classes at Cambridge. Alan Turing found the pace slow and classes boring. He graduated in 1934 and wrote a paper for the *Proceedings of the London Mathematical Society* describing a calculating machine that could solve any problem using binary digits. His paper laid the foundation for the binary memory used in all modern computers.

Turing didn't have to be bored for long. When England declared war on Germany in 1939, he joined a covert project still largely classified under Britain's Official Secrets Act. It was the ULTRA project, Britain's effort to crack the Germans' military code.

A Polish engineer who worked in a German factory before he was fired for being Jewish fled to France and rebuilt from memory the signaling device the factory produced. British agents helped him escape in exchange for it, an early version of the German coding device called the Enigma. It used three or four rotors to vary code keys used for that day's messages, as well as a plugboard that increased the code's possible combinations. In 1939, the Germans increased the rotors to eight.

The British cryptanalyst I. J. Good said Enigma could produce 10^{23} possible code combinations. No human team could decipher the combination for that day's messages within a reasonable time, and the Germans might change combinations three times a day. Later, the Germans switched to a more sophisticated code called the Fish, which used *ten* rotors.

Turing headed the top-secret code-cracking department, housed outside the town of Bletchley. He was a marathon runner, a man of sloppy habits with the engaging ability to laugh at himself, a homosexual who kept his proclivities secret.

"In discussions he was excitable and his voice would rise to a high pitch," recalled I. J. Good.

Between sentences he had a habit of saying "Ah-ah-ah-ah-ah. . . . ," which made it difficult to interrupt his line of thought, or even to have a line of thought of one's own! In the first week of June each year he would get a bad attack of hay fever, and he would cycle to the office wearing a service gas mask to screen the pollen. His bicycle had a fault; the chain would come off at regular intervals. Instead of having it mended he would count the number of times the pedals went round and would get off the bicycle in time to adjust the chain by hand. Another of his eccentricities was that he chained his mug to the radiator pipes to prevent its being stolen. [When someone actually went through the trouble of picking the lock and stealing it, Turing was outraged.]

When he attacked a problem he liked to start from first principles, and he was rarely influenced by received opinion.

By 1940, the group broke Enigma's code with the Bombe, a bronze-colored column about eight feet high, with wheels corresponding to Enigma's rotors. The staff nicknamed it "the Bronze Goddess" and "the oracle of Bletchley." It worked by electromechanical relays and was limited in what it could do.

The Bronze Goddess might have unraveled Enigma, but she found decoding the Fish too slippery a problem. To reel Fish in, the group needed a Colossus, a more advanced electromechanical calculator. They built the first Colossus in 1943.

Colossus had about 1,500 vacuum tubes and used punched paper tape for programming. Members of the Women's Royal Naval Service (Wrens) stood at toggle switches as a cryptoanalyst shouted programming instructions above the roar of clicking relays. Wrens worked as machine operators for the more powerful Colossus II, which had 2,500 vacuum tubes. Most of the pioneer computer projects used women operators to grind through equations or help program the machine, just as women did the laborious data processing on Hollerith machines.

The Nazis were also carrying out computer research. Werner von Braun, inventor of rockets that blasted much of London and its inhabitants to bits, had an electrical engineer on his team, Helmut Hoelzer, who built a fully electronic analog computer in 1941. Von Braun also used the services of the mathematician Alwin Walther, head of an influential research institute, who wanted to develop automated computation.

One German worked largely alone in constructing computers. The Third Reich wasn't interested in Konrad Zuse—he was only an eccentric who built relay computers in his parents' living room in Berlin. When Zuse became a soldier in 1939, a calculator manufacturer wrote Zuse's major, asking that Zuse be released to work on a computer for aircraft design calculations. Recalled Zuse, "My major looked at this letter and said, 'I don't understand that. The German aircraft is the best in the world. I don't see what to calculate further on.'" He did not release Zuse.

But *someone* appreciated Zuse. When the research institute head Walther heard of him, he visited Zuse in 1942 and saw his third computer, the Z3, hidden in a cellar to protect it from bombing raids.

"We immediately recognized the unique nature of this utterly unconventional, forward-looking, valuable development," wrote Walther's assistant. The Z3 incorporated advances Walther hadn't dreamed of, such as a binary system and mechanical switching elements. Fortunately, Zuse didn't use vacuum tubes, and he didn't like Walther.

The Reich was crippled by an understandable lack of collaboration with the countries at the forefront of computer research, Britain and the United States. It also suffered from government indifference. Apparently, other officers besides Zuse's major couldn't see the value of a machine that didn't drop bombs or shoot bullets. According to Walther's assistant, Walther's request to work on automated computation was dismissed as "superfluous" by "shortsighted and uncoordinated" Nazi army authorities with a "contemptuous" attitude. When the Reich learned of Howard Aiken's Mark I computer two years later, the supreme command demanded to know why

Walther wasn't working on a computer, too. Walther simply pulled out a copy of the army's refusal letter from the previous year.

By the time the Reich's errand boy stomped into Walther's office, Mark I's relays were clattering up a storm in Aiken's lab, staffed by U.S. naval personnel.

The retired naval commodore Grace Hopper, who worked on Aiken's Mark I and Mark II computers, recalled years later that despite his bad temper and sarcastic wit, the staff was devoted to him, slaving twenty-four hours a day. Their loyalty was tested one dangerous night when they got a hurricane warning that would have sent less dedicated workers running home. Instead, they stayed to finish the job, then formed a human chain and pulled each other from tree to tree until they got home.

Harvard's Mark I, the first electromechanical binary computer built in the States, was fifty-one feet long and eight feet tall, and contained over five hundred miles of wiring. The Mark I could do a multiplication in six seconds. It was close, very close, to the first modern electronic computer. In fact, it was only a few hundred miles away.

About the same time Aiken was peddling his dream, John W. Mauchly of the Moore School of Engineering at the University of Pennsylvania, about 280 miles southwest of Harvard, noticed that the vacuum tubes that astronomers used to count cosmic rays could measure a million counts a second. He wondered if vacuum tubes linked to electrical circuits could create a lightning-fast calculating machine able to compute complex weather patterns or ballistics problems. Colleagues laughed at him.

"I got the same answer," he said. " 'No. Vacuum tubes are so poor, unreliable. They're always burning out.' . . . But there was an exception, and wouldn't you just know, of course—the exception was a student. . . . He said, 'Yes. I don't see anything wrong with what you're talking about, John. You could do everything you're saying.' . . . If it hadn't been for J. Presper Eckert, I don't know what would have happened next."

Eckert headed a group of baby-faced engineers in the classified PX project, which used IBM punch card equipment and Bell Telephone relays. The 1943 project sprang from the Army's need to quickly figure artillery trajectories and bombing tables. Eckert and Mauchly started the PX project with a $61,-700 Army grant despite powerful opposition from MIT's Vannevar Bush, who opposed them partly because MIT and Harvard dominated computer research and partly because Bush believed in analog computers, while Eckert and Mauchly wanted to go digital. Howard Aiken also opposed their project, being quoted as saying, "There will never be enough problems, enough work, for more than one or two of these computers."

"They were the rich guys up there who did everything the hard way, as far as we were concerned," said Eckert about the Massachusetts mob. He and Mauchly imagined a machine that would use vacuum tubes in a "flip-flop" arrangement; each pair of vacuum tubes would be wired so that only one tube could be on at a time. When tube A was on, the flip-flop would be in its "1" state. When tube B was on, the flip-flop would be in its "0" state.

Less than two years later, an Italian mob strung up from a lamp post the bodies of Benito Mussolini and his mistress. Hitler's body smoldered in his bunker. In Philadelphia, the gleaming metallic body of another type of beast hummed, then died, hummed, then died again. The creature was a hundred feet long, ten feet high, three feet wide. It had about 18,000 vacuum tubes and 1,500 relays. It broke down almost every day. It was unlike anything the world had ever seen before, and its creators gave it a name the world had never heard before: Electronic Numerical Integrator and Computer (ENIAC).

ENIAC was two thousand times faster than the Harvard

Mark I. A calculation that took Mark I six seconds to do took ENIAC 2.8 milliseconds. ENIAC cost almost $500,000 to build. The staff programmed it by setting thousands of switches by hand. To an outsider, it might look like Frankenstein, but to Eckert and Mauchly, it was Galatea.

While power first surged through ENIAC's wires, haggard Berliners rummaged in trash cans for food. Konrad Zuse had smuggled his fourth computer, the Z4, to southern Bavaria, where it survived the war. The day before U.S. troops marched into Walther's institute at Darmstadt, Walther burned his papers, but occupation forces still found some German technology worth appropriating, including magnetic storage devices that evolved into the modern computer's magnetic memory.

With a Cold War chill hissing down its halls, the Pentagon wasted no time basking in new friendships with former Nazis. Both the rocket scientist Wernher von Braun and the analog computer researcher Helmut Hoelzer got jobs building rockets for the U.S. government. Hoelzer went on to help develop the Hermes rocket and NASA space program.

The United States was equally quick to ease its Stalinist comrades out the door. When the Soviet Union's purchasing commission wrote to the Moore School on April 5, 1946, saying, "We would appreciate your advising us as to whether you can accept our order for manufacturing the Robot Calculator," the response was silence. His marriages with both the Nazis and the Allies having ended in bloody divorce, and perhaps hoping the third time was a charm, Stalin pledged his troth to mainland China.

With the Second World War finally over, computer researchers realized that something this powerful would fill a vital civilian need. They rushed to stake their claim in history in order to ensure immortality and to patent all they could in order to ensure their fortunes. John V. Atanasoff was a central figure in the ensuing bitterness. His life story could be titled "What Might Have Been."

Like Zuse, Atanasoff was a loner. Unlike Mauchly and Eckert, he never received major funding for the only research field that was expensive from the start. Perhaps being out in the rural Midwest had something to do with it. He was a physicist at Iowa State College, now Iowa State University.

"Looking over the 1936 art in computing, I had become convinced that a new computer should provide for a much larger retention of data," he later wrote. "I had a few ideas, but nothing seemed to 'jell.' " Peers thought his ideas wild, and he felt suffocated between a heavy teaching load and his obsession.

"The winter of 1937 was a desperate one for me because I had this problem and I had outlined my objectives but nothing was happening," he said. "As the winter deepened, my despair grew. . . . I was just unhappy to an extreme degree, and at that time I did something that I had done on such occasions—I don't do it anymore—I went out to my automobile, got in and started driving over the good highways of Iowa at a high rate of speed."

He drove for hours, from Ames, over the Mississippi River, and into Illinois, turning down a Rock Island country road where tavern lights promised shelter from the cold.

"I had a very heavy coat, and hung it up, and sat down and ordered a drink, and as the delivery of the drink was made, I realized that I was no longer so nervous and my thoughts turned again to computing machines," he recalled. "Things seemed to be good and cool and quiet. There were not many people in the tavern, and the waitress didn't bother me particularly with repetitive offers of drinks.

"During that evening in the Illinois roadhouse, I made four decisions for my computer project. 1. I would use electricity and electronics as the media for the computer. 2. In spite of custom, I would use base-2 numbers (binary) for my computer. 3. I would use condensers for memory, but 'regenerate' to avoid lapse [use condensers that would retain an electrical charge without 'leaking' any of it when the computer's power was turned off]. 4. I would compute by direct logical action, not by enumeration."

Unaware of the classified Colossus project and other break-throughs, Atanasoff built an analyzer containing thirteen vacuum tubes. By the spring of 1939, he was confident enough of his work to apply for a grant and hired the electrical engineering student Clifford E. Berry as his assistant.

"Clifford E. Berry (CEB) was one of the best things that could have happened to the project," said Atanasoff. "He had vision and inventive skills."

They worked on the ABC (Atanasoff Berry Computer) in relative isolation. "I knew of no one who had essayed such a project, and my prospects filled me with foreboding as well as joy," said Atanasoff. In 1941, Mauchly visited Atanasoff, saw his machine, and later wrote him, "A number of different ideas have come to me anent computing circuits—some of which are more or less hybrids, combining your methods with other things, and some of which are nothing like your machine. The question in my mind is this: Is there any objection, from your point of view, to my building some sort of computer which incorporates some of the features of your machine?"

Atanasoff asked Mauchly to keep the ABC work confidential until it was patented, but the patent process got fouled up indefinitely. Mauchly teamed with Eckert and started on ENIAC.

The undergraduate Robert Mather, who worked for Atanasoff for fifty cents an hour, later speculated on why the ABC project failed.

"Probably the greatest fault with the computer project was that it was seriously underfunded," wrote Mather. "There were no funds that would have carried the project through the debugging stage and into useful application."

He remembered Clifford Berry as a gentle man.

"Looking back, I know I must have been irritating at times in spite of my great eagerness to please, and yet I recall no time at which Cliff expressed irritation," he wrote. "I always left with the impression that he respected and trusted me."

Despite a tight budget and tiny staff, they built the ABC, a digital electronic computer designed to solve up to thirty linear equations. It was small—a photograph shows it to be about the size of a large desk. It was never fully operational.

Mather left in 1942, the same year Berry married Atanasoff's secretary and moved to Pasadena, and Atanasoff went to Washington, D.C., to work for the Naval Ordnance Laboratory.

As the ABC gathered dust, the military-industrial complex skittered about the ENIAC and its implications with a mixture of fear and desire, like the apes confronted by the monolith in the movie *2001*. A company venturing into the unmapped waters of the computer age might haul in enormous profits. Then again, it might sink in red ink for marketing a machine no one wanted.

Even IBM pulled back from the potential Charybdis of computer marketing. Thomas Watson, Sr., was concerned that the company might hemorrhage money into a possibly enormous failure. There's a legend that IBM ordered a study in the early 1950s to determine whether a market existed for computers. The study concluded that in the next ten years the U.S. market might buy five computers, so IBM didn't tackle the computer market until relatively late.

Some who tell the tale today seem to enjoy recounting IBM's blunder. Nothing is as sure in hindsight as the inevitability of success, but in 1947 anyone who assumed computers would be hotter than Frank Sinatra would have had to have vacuum tubes for brains. In an era when many homes didn't have telephones or indoor water closets, when a company priding itself on the latest in technology might show off a single photostat machine, the market for computers was a dark puzzle indeed. A marketing director would have to answer hard questions: Who would be willing to pay for a machine likely to overrun initial cost estimates by more than 200 percent? Who wanted a machine that spent most of its time breaking down and needed a twenty-four hour staff to keep it running? Who had room for a machine requiring up to 3,000 cubic feet, its own air-conditioning system, and its own power supply? Any firm serious about the computer market would have to train legions of factory workers, researchers, and salesmen from scratch. It couldn't hire someone with a computer science degree, because in 1947 such degrees didn't exist.

So when Mauchly and Eckert asked for more research funds, Watson turned them down; they bolted, starting their own company, UNIVAC. UNIVAC had a lead of several years over the competition, but soon teetered on the verge of bankruptcy. Things looked up when the firm hired a manager who began pulling them back into the black, but he died in an airplane crash and UNIVAC sold out to Remington Rand, later Sperry Rand.

Everyone underestimated the market's ravenous appetite for computers of increasing speed and memory. Even the mathematician John von Neumann, who helped Mauchly and Eckert design ENIAC's successors, predicted that a computer would never need more than 10,000 binary words of memory to do a problem, and that 20,000 binary words would be more than enough for any machine.

Nevertheless, in 1950, Remington Rand unveiled UNIVAC, a formidable machine against which to compete. IBM soon built an electronic-electromechanical, stored-program digital computer that took up 1,500 square feet, and its salesmen began knocking on Pentagon doors to see what the military was willing to pay for. By 1954, IBM was definitely interested in computers, but Mauchly and Eckert had filed major patents whose validity depended on the originality of their ideas. That was when patent lawyers pulled Atanasoff in from offstage.

"On June 15, 1954, we received a visit from A. J. Etienne, who was a patent attorney for IBM," wrote Atanasoff. "Etienne announced his purpose by saying in substance, 'If you will help us, we will break the Mauchly-Eckert computer patent; it was derived from you.'"

Atanasoff was shocked. He recalled Mauchly saying he was building a computer that was different from the ABC. Officials from Datamatic, Sperry Rand, and the Burroughs Corporation also visited Atanasoff, all very interested in the ABC project. But he had left the ABC twelve years earlier and had lost his files on it.

During the morass of litigation, Atanasoff testified in a lawsuit between Honeywell and Sperry Rand, and the judge ruled him the creator of the first modern electronic digital computer. But judicial wisdom may not embrace the technical expertise to compare ABC and ENIAC, so the controversy drags on.

The computer historian Nancy Stern, an authority on the controversy, concluded that credit for the world's first modern electronic computer goes to Mauchly and Eckert. After all, said Stern, Mauchly thought of a vacuum tube electronic digital computer in the 1930s, and the ABC had little influence on ENIAC's design. Besides, the ENIAC worked; the ABC didn't.

"Like Babbage, Atanasoff never finished his work," wrote Stern. "Hence, to consider him an inventor of the first electronic digital computer is, I believe, an overstatement." Others disagree, saying Mauchly stole ideas from Atanasoff, whose historical importance has been ignored.

The ABC had a humble demise. When Robert Stewart was

a graduate physics student at Iowa State College in 1948, the department head told him to clean out a deserted lab room. Stewart entered to find "an unusual piece of equipment that involved motor-driven elements and vacuum-tube circuitry."

"The usable parts were returned to stock; the balance of the machine went to the loading dock to be hauled off with other trash," wrote Stewart. "Thus the ABC died, unheralded, ingloriously, and in a sense unnecessarily. Sic transit gloria."

In 1963, a mysterious death ended the role of another actor in computer history.

"Late in 1963," wrote Atanasoff, "I was overwhelmed to get a letter from Jean Berry, saying that Clifford had resigned his position, taken a place with a company in Long Island, and died one night at his apartment." A landlord found Clifford Berry dead with a plastic bag over his head. Four years later, Atanasoff investigated the gentle engineer's death.

"CEB's death was not natural," wrote Atanasoff. "He had been found in bed with a plastic sack over his head but with his bedclothes smoothly over his arms, which were by his sides. An autopsy revealed that his brain plasma had 0.12 percent alcohol content, which would have permitted him to drive a car in some jurisdictions. He had been taking Dilantin because of recent epilepsy, and so his blood and brain were carefully examined for this and other drugs; none were found. Suicide, said the authorities." Atanasoff didn't believe it. When he told what he'd discovered to Jean Berry, Clifford's widow, she didn't believe it, either.

"[Atanasoff] told me that the landlord had torn the plastic bag off Cliff's face with no difficulty," wrote Mrs. Berry. "When I told a physician what I knew, he said that Cliff could not possibly have killed himself—he was murdered: 'It's like trying to hold your breath; you can't.' . . . Atanasoff has referred to Berry's death as 'foul play.' From the information I have, I believe him."

The patent litigation rumbled on. Eckert and Mauchly's collaboration with the mathematician John von Neumann went sour, especially after von Neumann published a paper outlining how a computer should be designed, a paper incorporating much of what he learned in conversations with the ENIAC team. He published it before Eckert and Mauchly applied for patents, and that paper may have helped cost Eckert and Mauchly their patent rights and a fortune that could have been worth billions.

Von Neumann contributed significantly to early computer design when he worked with Mauchly and Eckert on the 1952 EDVAC project, but where his contributions leave off and those of others begin forms a vast gray area. Von Neumann, a joyous man with a Kewpie-doll face and a phenomenal mind, did not have a reputation for declining credit when credit wasn't due. His fame grew to such an extent that computers were often called "von Neumann machines," and Eckert's dislike of him grew with it. Eckert thought von Neumann brilliant but amoral, as blasé about taking credit for others' work as he was about drinking one of his famous martinis, rumored to be pure gin.

Across the ocean, another computer pioneer who might have interested the patent lawyers was as unreachable as Clifford Berry, and for the same reason. Alan Turing, who conceived of the binary computer yet never fixed his bicycle chain, suffered an equally tragic death, but not before laying the foundation for the British computer industry. His ACE (Automatic Computing Engine) report, finished in 1945, set forth the basics needed for a comprehensive, efficient British computer. The ACE report helped push the government to support computer research. Turing also described a theoretical invention now famous as the Turing machine, a universal computer capable of doing anything another machine—or even, potentially, the human mind—can do. Launching from this into philosophy,

Turing confronted the question "Can a computer think?" with a scenario called the Turing test: if someone questioning both a person and a computer can't decide on the basis of written replies which one is human, then "fair play" obliges one to accept that the machine *does* think. Why? Because we have no way of knowing if a *person* is thinking except by his or her responses, and what reason is there for imposing different criteria on a machine?

Turing's mind was as free as his spirit, as indifferent to the borders between mathematics and philosophy, between the computer as tool and as reflection of our minds, as he was to social convention. But some free spirits get crushed. This happened to Turing.

During Yuletide of 1951, he met an unemployed young man and took him home. He was burgled by a friend of his companion, and when he reported the burglary, he ended up confessing his sexual habits to police. Authorities charged Turing with the crime of homosexuality. He pled guilty and was forced to submit to hormone therapy designed to suppress his sexual urges. In 1954, he carried out a "desert island" experiment—a hobby of his to concoct poisons from common household materials. This time he created potassium cyanide, took it, and died.

The computer universe continued expanding without him. In the market's shark-infested seas, IBM was bigger and hungrier than its competitors, who were banished to the coterie of insignificant rivals known as the Seven Dwarfs, with IBM gaining the ironic nickname Snow White. Thomas Watson, Sr., had doubts about computers, but his son, Thomas Watson, Jr., pushed the company to take the risk. IBM marketed its first mass-produced high-performance computer, the 701, in 1953. It was called the Defense Calculator and was used mainly by the military.

The 701's design group of thirty-five engineers and scientists set up shop on the third floor of a Poughkeepsie tie factory.

They later moved to a former supermarket whose roof leaked tar on hot days, splattering the design drawings. Engineers just scraped off the tar and kept on drawing, eventually manufacturing twenty 701s, computers that could be packed in boxes small enough to fit in an elevator. The 701 used magnetic tape, a new sight to factory workers.

"The first shipment came in a box like cellophane tape," remembered an IBM employee. The production manager "was called down to the inspection area where a man had unrolled about a 100 feet of tape on the floor. 'What's the matter?' [the manager] asked. 'It's not good,' the inspector answered. 'There's no adhesive on the back.' "

By 1957, IBM had an improved computer, the 704, and installed it at MIT, where students yearned to touch it but were shooed away by the 704's priests-caretakers. Within a few years, the youths swarmed over a computer built and discarded by Lincoln Labs, the TX-0, that used transistors instead of vacuum tubes. Transistors were smaller and tougher than vacuum tubes, an advance as major as the microcircuits that would one day replace transistors. By now, digital computers were triumphing over analogs, which were less accurate and became almost extinct.

The MIT computer room habitués explored the TX-0's guts, taking its circuits out for a spin, devising ever more elegant programs. They were called "computer bums" and later "hackers." The hackers joyously got hold of a PDP-1 a few years later, a minicomputer manufactured by a new company, Digital Equipment Corporation (DEC). The PDP-1 was about the size of three refrigerators and was built to be explored. It cost $120,000 retail, one of the first computers a medium-sized company could afford.

By the early sixties, the computer market had become a free-for-all where engineers sweated out marathon building sessions to edge out rivals, their machines soon made obsolete by other competitors. The modern computer's midwives went their separate ways; tragedies aside, the fifties and sixties were glory days for that new species—the computer scientist. Computer research was a vast uncharted ocean, and helmsmen familiar with its mysteries could demand their price. John von Neumann became a well-paid industry and government consultant. Mauchly started a computer consulting business whose stock skyrocketed before plummeting to ruin. He retired to a Pennsylvania farm, selling off land to pay debts. Eckert retired from Sperry Univac to a posh Pennsylvania suburb. Thomas Watson, Jr., inherited his father's position as IBM president.

Today, computer business means greater speed, faster memory, overnight obsolescence, lawsuits, countersuits, firms springing up like mushrooms after thunderstorms and shriveling just as quickly. Computer science has left mathematics and electrical engineering to become its own field, no longer dominated by inventors and greasy-haired hackers, but by students who like to go home for dinner and by pleasant company men who wear ties.

"Ten years ago, [computing] was tremendous, it was something very special," recalled George Sintchak, an instrumentation project engineer at Brookhaven National Laboratory in 1986. "Now there are a couple of million [computers] out there. The mystique has been taken away. A computer has become an appliance." He spoke with regret, as if something precious had been lost. And perhaps something was.

But something more precious was gained. Californians soldering "home brew" computers in their garages and crying, "Power to the people!" toppled the ministers of information and started the personal-computer revolution. As computers evolved from the esoteric to the commonplace, their cost plunged and their size shrank. Today, you might see an abacus used as a paperweight or a slide rule used as a tie clip, but the computer will be in the thick of battle: a hand calculator under a mountain of bills, a running dishwasher, a stereo radiating music, the blinking screen of a desktop computer.

Computers are so widespread now that we hardly notice them, infiltrating our lives so thoroughly that they're subjects of common jokes and legends. Like Orpheus, the tales rise from the yellowing corpses of news clippings, singing with an inner music that captures the hearer's heart and makes the story immortal.

THE CYBERNETIC
GODS

Grown men banged their heads on desks and cried. Admirals dissolved into khakied masses of frustration. Finally, naval brass visited the office of the cybernetics pioneer Norbert Wiener. A top-secret computer he designed was on the blink, stranding a battleship in the middle of the Pacific. Would he help?

While they described the problem, Wiener laced his fingers behind his head and closed his eyes, leaning back in his chair. He thought for a moment, then said, "Remove the computer's T12X panel. Behind it you'll find a wire eaten through by a mouse. Change the wire."

The navy men eyed each other, then turned again as Wiener cleared his throat.

"It will be a gray mouse, I believe," he added.

Having no other choice, they radioed the ship with Wiener's instructions. Three hours later the ship radioed back, "Panel removed. Wire replaced. Problem solved. Note: mouse was gray."

Norbert Wiener is one of the cybernetic gods who carried the computer out of dreams and into reality. In fact, he coined the word "cybernetics" from the Greek *kybernetes,* meaning "steersman." Just as the human brain steers the body's responses, the cybernetic brain steers the computer. Cybernetics is the science of designing machines that mimic human abilities.

Wiener was an owlish, heavy-set man whose watery dark eyes looked huge behind his thick glasses. If any of the legends that grew up around him are true, then the adage "God protects fools and children" could be extended to "God protects fools, children, and Norbert."

For one thing, legend says that Wiener liked to read while walking to work. He would often be seen walking by—or rather, through—the rushing traffic on Massachusetts Avenue, his face plastered in a book, oblivious to cars blaring past.

He even devised a way to get to his office without having to look where he was going. He used the maze solution, walking with his left hand touching the left wall. Eventually, he traced past all the walls until he reached the outside, or his office.

One day, Wiener was trundling down the hall in his usual bookish daze, trailing his left hand along the wall. A colleague sitting at his desk with his door open was startled when Wiener walked in, ignored his greeting, and perambulated around the office, trailing his hand along the walls. Wiener completed the circumscription and wandered out without a word.

It's something of a miracle that Wiener could find his way home. In fact, in one story that was a major problem. In it, the Wieners were moving. Starting a month before the big day, his wife told him every morning during breakfast, "Now, Norbert, we're moving soon, so remember on moving day that you won't live here anymore, but at the new address."

Moving day finally came. Wiener returned from work to the old address, only to find an empty house. He immediately suspected something was wrong. He remembered vague reminders about a new address. Walking up and down the sidewalk in front of his old house, he saw a little girl and asked, "Excuse me, but do you know where the famous mathematician Norbert Wiener lives?"

"Yes I do, Daddy," she replied. "Mommy sent me to take you home."*

John von Neumann, Wiener's peer and occasional collaborator in creating the modern computer, was another cybernetic god. His fellow mathematician Jacob Bronowski called von Neumann "the cleverest man I ever knew, without exception," and Bronowski's circle included Enrico Fermi and Niels Bohr.

Like those about Wiener, anecdotes about von Neumann show him as someone who was on the spacey side. For instance, his wife was sick once and confined to bed, so she asked him to go downstairs and get her a drink of water. She heard him clatter down the steps to the kitchen, rattle around for about ten minutes, then clatter back up the stairs and ask, "Darling, where do we keep the glasses?" They'd lived there for seventeen years.

As cybernetic gods go, Wiener and von Neumann might have both been spacey, but in other respects they diverge. Wiener was as concerned about philosophy, religion, and social values as he was with computers. Von Neumann didn't seem concerned about anything, his large dark eyes alight with joy while Wiener's were anxious and brooding. Wiener slugged through mathematical thickets, moaning to friends about how impossible they were, fighting his way to a solution because the abyss of failure frightened him. In contrast, von Neumann romped through mathematical problems with delight, as if everything were a game without consequences.

In fact, von Neumann loved all kinds of games: word games,

---

*"I have a small correction/addition to the Norbert Wiener story about him losing his family," wrote Betsy Perry by electronic mail. "An unfortunate young man once told the story in [Peggy Wiener Kennedy's] presence, and she froze him with a stare, saying, 'Father may have been absent-minded, but he always knew who we were.'"

guessing games, bets, puzzles, wearing paper hats at parties. He was as rambunctious as a kid; everyone called him Johnny. Entranced by clever children's toys, he on one occasion battled a five-year-old over who'd be the first to play with some interlinking building blocks. It isn't surprising that he was the creator of game theory.*

Johnny von Neumann combined a child's curiosity with an adolescent's emotional age, a hedonist's amoral passions, and a photographic memory. Once, when challenged, he astonished friends at a party by reciting *A Tale of Two Cities* for fifteen minutes until they begged him to stop. He hadn't read the book in twenty years. He also reputedly had one of the world's largest memorized collections of dirty limericks.

Of course, his real gift was his almost supernatural grasp of mathematics, by which he immediately perceived difficulties in computer science and instantly conceived original solutions. His Princeton students found him an inspiring but incomprehensible lecturer; he'd write equations on the board with one hand and erase them with the other before anyone had a chance to copy them down. Once he showed up for class in formal evening dress, with his bow tie askew and his eyes half closed, as if he'd been up all night partying—which he had.

Johnny von Neumann's ability to solve complex equations rapidly impressed even his peers, who were no slouches themselves. In one story, a colleague gave von Neumann a mathematical puzzle: "You have two trains coming at each other at x miles an hour, and a bird flies back and forth between them. If the trains start y miles apart, how far does the bird fly until it's squashed?"

Von Neumann responded instantly with the right answer.

"Very good!" his friend said. "You know, most people don't

*Game theory is a mathematical theory dealing with strategies to maximize wins and minimize losses. In the real world, it offers solutions in decision-making problems.

figure out the short cut to solving that problem. Instead, they go through the long process of trying to sum up the infinite series." Confused, von Neumann replied, "But that's what I did."

Friends would pit von Neumann against a computer to figure an involved equation, and he'd usually finish first. Supposedly, once he was working as a consultant for a major corporation designing a new computer. He insisted on being left alone in a room with the prototype for an afternoon. When he came out, the staff asked if the machine was good enough to hit the assembly line.

"No," he said. "Not good enough. Work on it some more."

They went back to work, and a week later he returned to test the revised prototype. He spent another afternoon with the machine behind closed doors, then burst out to announce, "Still not good enough," and left. The staff again returned to the drawing board.

He returned the next week, locked himself in the room with the prototype, finally came out, and said, "All right, you can start mass production."

"How do you decide when it's good enough for that?" someone asked.

"When it can beat me," he replied.

In contrast to von Neumann, the British computer pioneer Alan Turing was a laconic deity. Turing was a marathon runner who ran mental marathons as well, performing feats such as conceiving the binary numerical system used in all computers today. Though with people he could be aloof and cold, he seems to have kept in close contact with nature, especially the heavens. He used to set his clock at night by looking outside to see when a certain star slid behind a neighboring building, and once when he didn't have a watch and needed to know the time, he improvised a sundial.

Turing was a practical man who lived on the Spartan side,

but his view of practicality might strike other people as strange. For instance, he and a friend hit upon the perfect way to use those precious moments in chess during which one waits for the opponent to make his move.

They decided to combine chess with running. As soon as a player made his move, he had to run a frantic lap around the garden. If the other player hadn't made his move by then, the runner got an extra move. Of course, running too fast could leave a person so oxygen starved that he couldn't think, which would bungle even a free move, so the runner had to maintain a delicate balance between running like the wind and not getting winded. It is perhaps the only form of chess in which players build up their calves.

Like the rest of his divine pack, Turing had a few loose ends—in his gloves, for instance. During World War II, whenever he was sitting in a shelter during air raids, he taught himself how to knit and made himself a pair of gloves without using instructions or a pattern. However, when it came to finishing the fingers, he was stymied. The solution was beyond his reach, though it was right at his fingertips. Unwilling to waste good English wool, he bicycled in to work wearing the gloves, with yarn dangling from the ends. Finally, one of the women in his office felt sorry for him and knitted the glove fingers closed.

Turing was such a shabby dresser and peculiar-looking fellow that he was arrested once by the police. He had the suspicious habit during walks of sticking his head into bushes and hedgerows in order to study their leaves and blossoms. Someone who saw him doing this mistook him for a German spy and called the constables, who almost threw the head of the government's secret Nazi code-cracking unit into jail.

Turing tended to ignore convention. He didn't flout it; he just didn't care. As a subordinate in His Majesty's government, he was supposed to endure official rigmarole, but he often managed to sidestep it in his quiet way. Nothing illustrates this better than the tale of Turing and the Home Guard.

Turing grew intrigued with sharpshooting and decided he wanted to learn how to use a rifle, but to get rifle training he was required to join the Home Guard, whose officers were fond of holding pointless marching exercises that Turing suspected he'd find unexciting. Though he didn't see any point in bumbling about in formation, he still filled out the recruitment form.

However, he paused when he came to the question "Do you understand that by enrolling in the Home Guard you place yourself liable to military law?" He saw no good in agreeing, so he wrote "no."

He went into training and endured the parades long enough to become an excellent marksman. Having mastered what he wanted to learn, he stopped showing up for drills, to the consternation of his commanding officer. The officer sought Turing out and demanded to know why he wasn't showing up for drills. Turing replied that he didn't feel like it, since he'd already learned how to shoot a rifle.

"It's not your job to decide whether or not you'll attend drills," the commander yelled. "You're a soldier! You'll do what you're told!"

Turing's reply was something to the effect of "Oh, I don't think I'm a soldier, really."

This galled the officer, who decided threats would work when orders failed. "Don't you realize that you're under military law?" he snapped. "You must do what you're told, or face serious consequences."

Turing's reply was something like "Oh, I don't think I'm under military law, really."

"What do you mean?" the officer roared. "You signed the form! Why, I have your papers right here!" And he pulled them out, took a look, and got a surprise.

The head command decided that Turing was "improperly

enrolled" and wasn't part of the Home Guard, really. That got Turing off the hook.

Why did fledgling computer science draw such a gaggle of eccentrics? Perhaps because those who'd never paid much attention to rules and limits felt more comfortable exploring this realm without boundaries than did those who were used to having their world defined. Since a computer employs a language pared to the core of symbolic truth, programming drew people who loved linguistics, the sinuous way that language curls around truth to obscure or reveal it. Those who were in love with mathematics discovered in computer science a way to turn those abstract mathematical truths into power and beauty, to make them flesh. The discipline's novelty attracted mavericks, and its creativeness seduced them into staying. Also, companies were initially open-minded about whom they would consider for computer jobs, because it was hard to find employees in this unknown and intimidating field.

"Computer science education is big now; they give doctorates in it," recalled Robert W. Bemer, who began his programming career when many people considered electric typewriters the latest in high technology. "We didn't have any education of that type. We were apprentices. Early programming is where the story originated that if you looked in one ear and couldn't see daylight you could hire the person. . . . It seemed we were just taking personnel in off the streets.

"David Sayre's background was in crystallography; I was an ex-set-designer for the movies. I once decided to advertise for chess players because I thought they would be pretty good programmers; it worked very well. We even hired the U.S. chess champion, Arthur Bisguier. He mostly played chess and didn't do that much programming. I told that story on a train out to Chicago once, and somebody at the next table said, 'I'll send my nephew in—he is traveling around Europe with a guitar.'

"The nephew came in and announced himself as the chess champion of the French Riviera. I didn't know anything about that particular title, so I said, 'I can't disprove it, but would you mind playing a game with a fellow in here?' He said, 'Oh, no, I wouldn't mind.' I went to Bisguier and said, 'Hey, Art, we've got some guy out here who is the chess champion of the French Riviera. Would you play a game with him, even though it's not professional?' He said 'Yes' and came through the door. The guy's jaw dropped and he said, 'You can't fool me—that's Bisguier!' By the way, the champion of the French Riviera was Sid Noble. He turned out to be an excellent programmer."

Free spirits must have felt more at home in computer companies in those days, with some turning to spirits of another sort to lighten up grueling programming marathons, as Bemer described: "Programming for the 604, the CPC, and such was done with plugboards. To use a plugboard, you had a bunch of wires of different lengths—they were color-coded so you knew their lengths. In the CPC days we often had to run the computer around the clock. We needed cola to keep us awake, but cola isn't very good without rum. We kept the rum in the long green wires."

What most computer pioneers shared in those days, no matter how disparate their backgrounds, was a latent or full-blown mathematical ability. In fact, one popular legend has been ascribed to so many cybernetic gods that you could call it the story of the undergraduate with a thousand faces.

In it, the future cybernetic wonder arrives late at class to see five equations on the blackboard. He assumes they're homework and works on them over the weekend, returning Monday to tell his professor, "I was able to solve three, but the other two were just too tough." His instructor's amazed because those weren't homework problems, but famous "unprovable" theorems.

This story, as well as many other well-known sagas of cybernetic deities, originated in fields such as physics or electrical engineering. The tale of Charles Proteus Steinmetz is a good example. Steinmetz was Thomas Edison's competitor, a hunchbacked German immigrant whose twisted body didn't impede his boundless confidence. Edison discovered direct current (DC), whereas the bespectacled Steinmetz discovered alternating current (AC). He chomped cigars as relentlessly as he tackled electromagnetic enigmas and held spirited arguments with the likes of Albert Einstein.

As the story goes, a Long Island utility contacted Steinmetz because its major power plant kept shutting down. He told the staff to set up a cot and a pillow by the main generator, then went to the plant. He showed up with a piece of chalk, lay down on the cot, adjusted the pillow, and closed his eyes.

"All right, turn on the generator," he said. The generator rumbled into life. After a few seconds, Steinmetz said, "All right, turn it off." He got up, went to the generator, marked a panel with the chalk, and told the plant engineer, "The coil inside this panel is overwired. Remove about fifteen feet of wire, and your problem is solved."

They followed his instructions and solved the problem. Steinmetz then gave them a bill for $10,000. The plant manager's face flushed purple as he exclaimed, "How can you stick us with such a huge bill for doing almost nothing?"

"A nickel of that is for the chalk," replied Steinmetz. "The rest is for knowing which panel to mark."

This has parallels with the Wiener mouse story at the beginning of the chapter, as well as with another computer story about Seymour Cray, designer of the Cray supercomputer.

Company managers for a firm that owned a Cray computer called him to complain that it kept malfunctioning, that they couldn't figure out why, and that the problem had brought their company to a standstill. Cray visited the company computer room, listened as engineers described the computer's glit-ches, and ordered everyone out. He then locked the door and sat on a stool for two hours and twenty-six minutes. Finally he emerged from the room, pointed to the computer's schematic, said, "Change *this* wire," and returned to his home in Chip-pewa Falls, Minnesota. The engineers followed his advice, and the machine worked.

Legends about software masters of the universe are less common than other stories, perhaps because software came into its own as a high art only after hardware hackers established their turf. Donald Knuth is one of the world's foremost software legends, author of the landmark multivolume work *The Art of Computer Programming*. He follows in the tradition of cyber-netic gods by being rather unusual.

His accomplishments began in the eighth grade, when a Milwaukee candy manufacturer ran a contest in which who-ever could think of the most words that could be made out of "Ziegler's Giant Bar" would win a television set for his or her school.

"I told my parents I had a stomach ache so that I didn't have to go to school for two weeks," he recalled. "I spent all those two weeks with an unabridged dictionary finding all the words I could get from the specified letters. I wound up with about 4,500 words, and the judges had only 2,500 on their master list." Besides winning a television set for his school, Knuth won a Ziegler's Giant Bar for everyone in his class, ensuring his popularity.

Greater triumphs were yet to come. While still a high school senior, Knuth had his first national publication: "The Potrzebie System of Weights and Measures," published in *MAD* maga-zine. Such an achievement could have ignited a glorious career as a journalist, but Knuth's interests lay elsewhere. He applied to Valparaiso University, where he intended to major in music, and to Case Western Reserve, where he intended to major in physics. Case accepted him, so he ended up in physics, starting his journey into computer science.

Women are rarely stars in the constellation of gods. Though scores worked as programmers with early modern computers, and though increasing numbers are now going into the field, very few women have entered the pioneer Parthenon. An exception is the retired naval commodore Grace Murray Hopper, creator of COBOL (COmmon Business Oriented Language), one of the earliest computer languages, which is still in use. Hopper also worked on the Mark I and Mark II projects.

Despite her long career and many accomplishments, Hopper will most probably be remembered for her colorful story on the origin of the term "bug" to mean a minor computer malfunction in hardware or software. The diminutive mathematician, who's now in her eighties, has traveled throughout the United States on the lecture circuit and has often told the story, recalled here in an interview with Voice of America:

> That was back on Mark I. It was in 1945. We were building Mark II—and Mark II stopped. We finally located the failing relay and, inside the relay, beaten to death by the relay contact, was a moth about three inches long. So the operator got a pair of tweezers and carefully fished the bug out of the relay and put it in the log book. He put scotch tape over it and wrote, "First actual bug found." And the bug is still in the log book under the scotch tape and it is in the Museum of the Naval Surface Weapons Center at Dahlgren, Virginia.

Actually, as in many tales, the reality behind the bug is wrapped in a cocoon of mystery, but we do know that the term is pretty old. Again, it sprang from electrical engineering.

"I have the right principle and am on the right track, but time, hard work, and some good luck are necessary too," wrote

Thomas Edison to his representative in France in 1878. "The first step is an intuition, and comes with a burst, then difficulties arise—this thing gives out and then that—'Bugs'—as such little faults and difficulties are called—show themselves. . . ."

By 1889, the use of "bug" was common enough that the *Pall Mall Gazette* reported that Edison spent sleepless nights "discovering a 'bug' in his phonograph—an expression for solving a difficulty, and implying that some imaginary insect has secreted itself inside and is causing all the trouble."

A bug's a nice image for describing a problem that's usually much more elusive than your average moth. Even the simplest desktop terminal is the result of the efforts of hundreds of people, all of whom made their individual contributions. The engineers, scientists, inventors, and programmers who swarmed over the early machines have been succeeded by more engineers, scientists, and programmers swarming around newer machines. The result is a creation that no one totally understands.

According to legend, only a cybernetic god has the supreme intuition and the sheer power of knowledge to exorcise especially demonic bugs. One tale of such prowess features Marvin Minsky, founder of MIT's Artificial Intelligence Laboratory. One day, he wandered into a computer room where he saw a frustrated student whacking the side of a malfunctioning computer.

Appalled, Minsky exclaimed, "You can't fix a computer without knowing what's wrong with it!" Then he walked over and whacked the computer in the same place.

It started working again.

THE HACKER'S
UNIVERSE

The mobs of the twenty-first-century French revolt were massacring the intelligentsia by the truckload. Revolutionaries dragged their latest victims to the guillotine: a priest, a lawyer, and a systems programmer.

As the priest fell to his knees, his executioners asked, "How would you like to go, face up or face down?"

Trembling, he replied, "I'd like to go face up, so I can look for my Maker."

They shoved him onto the bench, snapped the pillory around his neck, and pulled the lever. The blade hissed down, but stopped as it touched his Adam's apple. The crowd cried out, "It's a miracle!"

"It is miraculous," the executioners said. "We must let him go!" So they did.

Then they dragged the lawyer up to the bench and asked him which way he'd like to face.

"Not wanting to break a precedent, I'll go face up," he coolly replied.

They snapped him into place and pulled the lever. The blade flashed again, and again frooze just a hair above his neck. The crowd gasped.

"Twice in one day, another miracle!" said the executioners. "We must let him go, too." And they did.

Now they dragged the systems programmer to the stage.
Asked which way he'd like to face, he said, "I'd like to go
face up to see how that mechanism works."
   They stuck him on the bench and put the pillory into
place, but before the executioner could pull the lever, the
engineer cried, "Wait! I see what the problem is! There's a
twisted line in the pulley!"

Computer fanatics have a different way of looking at the
world. It might be hard to understand someone whose idea of
the good life is spending eighteen hours a day in the computer
room and sleeping on the lounge room couch. That, however,
can be the vision of paradise for computer experts going
through their rite of passage, the fervid hacker* phase.

It's during this phase that the novice becomes obsessed with
the new worlds and powers the computer offers. Outsiders
might call the hacker's obsession a kind of color blindness; he is
able to see the blues and greens of analytical life but is blind to
the colors of passion. A hacker might argue that his merely
human spectrum of sight is now expanded into the ultraviolet
and infrared, into strange lands most people never see. It's like
being jolted into a realm as exotic as the Amazon, yet as starkly
majestic as the Antarctic. The hacker finds joy in creating programs that work, mastery in conquering the machine, and escape in marathon sessions of games such as Dungeons and
Dragons, linking dozens of players together through electronic
umbilical cords.

Over time, the computer can assume an almost human personality to the hacker. Take this student's description of an
early DEC computer called the PDP-11. The student trans-

---

*Because of the flood of computer viruses and other mean tricks, the word
"hacker" is taking on negative connotations. In this book, "hacker" is not intended
in a derogatory sense, but means someone who loves working with computers to the
point where his or her life revolves around it.

forms the PDP from a bunch of wires and chips into a frantic Buster Keaton:

> When Digital Equipment Corporation (DEC) first created the PDP-11, it didn't realize the mainframe was capable of things DEC hadn't foreseen. The creators made it with a function that is very fast and has certain interrupt levels, so the function runs around saying, "Oh, I'm running. I'm running a Level 5 job and here comes a Level 7 interrupt. That's okay, I'm more important. I'll keep on working here. Oh my God! A Level 2 interrupt. This guy must really want me." And runs up there.
>
> "What do you want?" he asks.
>
> And the program says, "Oh, ah, am I finished yet?"
>
> "No!" he yells, then runs back down to Level 5 and says to himself, "Okay, fine. I can start again right down here. Oh, I'm finished. Oh! I have this little Level 7 interrupt that I guess I should look at. Oh oh! It says my terminal is free so I can print things on it. Okay, I'll print such and such."
>
> There are certain higher levels of interrupt. If one interrupt hits the function as it's running along, it says, "Oh my God! The line current has dropped to 109 volts! I bet somebody has just flicked the switch, and I've only got 329 nanoseconds before the whole system goes down. That's okay. That gives me more than enough time to save all the registers, load them in the locations they should be in, this, that, and the other thing."
>
> So the function scurries around, does all this, says, "Ah! Whew, I've got a couple of nanoseconds, I guess I'll wait here until, you know, I go to sleep." So you flip off the switch and the thing is dead.
>
> When you flip the switch on the function jumps up and exclaims, "Oh my God! I'm over 109 volts. I must be on. Well, quick, load everything back up in the accumulators and start running again right where I was."

In another story, the computer shows human frustration and relief:

Speaker X: This is sworn by Ed, who was working for Grumman on microprocessor chips. Those little chips are really sensitive to static electricity. They were working in an office with rugs, which really build up static, and the console's responding automatically by typing responses as he's working with it. Some guy built up enough static electricity that when he touched the CPU chip he sent a small current through it. Killed the chip. Before the chip died, the last thing it typed out on the console was "fuck." This poor chip. "Fuck."

Speaker Y: Go look at the AI (artificial intelligence) lab. They have this old, decrepit console that monitors an output device and types out whatever it's doing. It's been there since time immemorial. One day it finally broke, and one of the last things that it says on the printout is "AH!" Someone scribbled on it, "Is this a sigh of relief?"

Sometimes the computer's an obsequious servant, and sometimes it's coldly indifferent to the programmer's needs, as in the legend of a low-priority program submitted at MIT in 1967. Staffers discovered the program in 1973 when they closed down the mainframe; it *still* hadn't run yet. The mainframe kept kicking the program down the queue for *six years* in favor of higher-priority jobs, while the person who submitted it languished day after day until he shuffled away in despair.

Despite the computer's occasional tyranny, the person in its thrall finds more pleasure with its company than in the company of boring and unpredictable humans. The cement-block computer room becomes a portal to another universe where a person is a hero, a leader, a teacher, a wizard, an adventurer, where one's friends share one's narrow but exhilarating existence, and may also share one's past as lonely outsiders in the messy world of human interaction. The hackers join in an electronic noosphere, merging souls through the circuits that extend across the nation, the continent, the ocean, the world, spiraling into infinity. Power! Freedom! Escape! Belonging!

The college hacker rises like a vampire when the sun goes down in order to invade the computer room during off-hours, between 10:00 P.M. and 5:00 A.M., when computer time is cheaper and the computer works faster because fewer people are using it. His alertness peaks during a cusp of the night when most people are deeply asleep. The electronic alchemy makes time fall away. He leans forward, his face inches from the computer screen, fingers a blur as he types without consciously thinking of what he is doing, a fusion of thought and action.

When his stomach rumbles, he orders a pizza, but by the time it's delivered he's lost again in the netherworld glowing greenly before him. He lets the pizza sit until the cheese congeals into an oleaginous consistency and the grease streaks cool into opaque white smears. He finally rips a cold slice from the cardboard box (box and pizza by now having the same texture) and chomps on it without tasting it, washing it down with a flat soda he got from the vending machine hours earlier.

Both his diet and his sleeping patterns go to hell. So does his body. He's sucked into a multihour computer confrontation that hackers call sportdeath, as he pushes his body to the limits in his mind duel with the machine. Stubble-faced and malodorous, his skin gleaming beneath fluorescent lights, he metamorphoses into a red-eyed cartilaginous creature crouched over the keyboard, claws raised, motionless as a preying mantis, transfixed by the terminal's evil eye. He may not be entirely happy with hackertude; in fact, computer jargon can be violent, expressing the programmer's frustration with balky machines.

"We speak with ease about a process being orphaned because its parent has been killed," noted Danny Sharpe of West Georgia College. "The message FATAL ERROR used to make me feel guilty, like I had hurt the machine somehow, but now I'm used to it and it doesn't bother me any more. Thousands of commands get aborted every day, but you don't see protesters on the steps of the computer center."

After more hours of searing his eyeballs in cathode rays, the thrall takes a nap on the student lounge's threadbare couch. He stretches his malnourished body along the worn cushions, which sag like twin sinkholes, pitted with cigarette burns and stained with coffee and pizza, settling weary bones around lumps that by now are as familiar to him as his own body, closing his burning eyes to fall instantly asleep.

But even in sleep his mind races along the computer's circuits, resurrecting jabbering, frenzied caricatures of the programs he has done and the programs he would like to do.

His eyes pop open an hour later. His brain, which hasn't slept at all, drags his enslaved body back to the keyboard. He fires mind and vestigial body hour after hour in sportdeath, pushing his reserves to the limit. Finally, numb with exhaustion, he and a few friends go out for breakfast.

Pulling on his jacket as they go down the stairs, he notices in an offhand way that pink is glimmering along the horizon. The cold air of dawn shocks his lungs as he hits the parking lot. Everyone squeezes into a friend's rusty Ford. They drive to a diner where the pancakes are filling and the coffee is bitter and hot. He attacks the meal, trading jokes, spacing out, easing into the cocoon of comradeship that wraps around his exhaustion like a soft blanket.

A buddy drops him off at his apartment as the paper boy throws the morning news onto dew-soaked lawns. The hacker unlocks the door, goes in, kicks off his shoes, and falls spread-eagle on the bare mattress, spiraling into the deepest sleep. He may get up by late afternoon in time to attend classes. Then again, he may not. Like many other hackers, he might lose interest in school and flunk, or drop out. School is no longer real. The real world begins at the doorway to the computer room.

His obsession changes the way the student thinks. For a short but intense time, he will look at the world through silicon-encrusted glasses, and he will think in the otherworldly plane of computer logic, a vision of reality satirized in this joke:

> A mathematician, a physicist, an engineer, and a computer scientist were asked to "prove" that all odd numbers are prime.
> The mathematician says, "Let's see. Three is a prime, five is a prime, and seven is a prime; therefore by mathematical deduction all odd numbers are prime."
> The physicist says, "Three is a prime, five is a prime, seven is a prime, nine is—well, I'll discard that as experimental error—eleven's a prime, thirteen's a prime, so empirical evidence indicates all odd numbers are prime."
> The engineer says, "Three is a prime, five is a prime, seven is a prime, nine is a prime, eleven is a prime." He's pleased with himself until the others tell him to go home.
> That leaves the computer scientist, who says, "Three's a prime, five's a prime, seven's a prime, seven's a prime, seven's a prime . . ."

Computer infatuation has caused at least one hospitalization. A young man whose obsession exploded into psychosis was admitted to Copenhagen's Nordvang Hospital in 1987. The eighteen-year-old spent twelve to sixteen hours a day in front of his computer, his thought processes turning into programming language. He woke up in the middle of the night thinking, "Line 10: go to the bathroom; Line 11 next." He told doctors that homo sapiens is only a machine and that no difference exists between the two. Psychologists examining him said, "He merged with the computer and afforded it supernatural qualities," until he was overwhelmed by insomnia and anxiety. One Danish computer expert described the typical obsessive hacker as a young man waking at mid-afternoon and working at his computer until four in the morning, who "drinks three liters of Coke and has no girlfriend."

The computer science professor Joseph Weizenbaum of

MIT became so concerned about computer obsession that he wrote a now famous description of it:

> Bright young men of disheveled appearance, often with sunken glowing eyes, can be seen sitting at computer consoles, their arms tensed and waiting to fire, their fingers already poised to strike at the buttons and keys on which their attention seems to be as riveted as a gambler's on the rolling dice. When not so transfixed, they often sit at tables strewn with computer printouts over which they pore like possessed students of a cabalistic text.
>
> They work until they nearly drop, twenty, thirty hours at a time. Their food, if they arrange it, is brought to them: coffee, Cokes, sandwiches. If possible, they sleep on cots near the computer. But only for a few hours—then back to the console or the printouts. Their rumpled clothes, their unwashed and unshaven faces, and their uncombed hair all testify that they are oblivious to their bodies and to the world in which they move. They exist, at least when so engaged, only through and for the computers. These are computer bums, compulsive programmers. They are an international phenomenon.

Weizenbaum's description makes those in the throes of hackertude sound like Renfield, thrall of Dracula, or like the pot-crazed piano player in the U.S. government propaganda movie *Reefer Madness*. The hacker's increasingly bizarre circadian habits draw him farther and farther from the lives of everyday people, and closer to hard-core hackers. He eventually breaks off into a tiny island of hackerdom, the land of Us, while the rest of humanity lives on the distant continent of Them.

A hacker who completely loses touch with Them might evolve into a social oddity who'd draw sympathy if he weren't so hilarious. This notorious creature waddles through the streets squinting and picking his nose, an example of what happens when computer addiction goes too far. The pockets of his petroleum-based white shirts are always blotted with ink, and his trouser cuffs are always three inches short. His voice makes cats howl. You know his name. Perhaps even in Neanderthal days, artists would take time out from sketching bison on cave walls to draw pictographs of a squint-eyed guy with big ears, horrible skin, and a wedgied loincloth. Ecce homo nerd.

"Silicon Valley is to nerds what Hollywood is to actors," wrote the Knight-Ridder reporter Stephen G. Bloom in an August 1987 article. Nerd empowerment is so strong there that clubs with names such as Nerds Night Out flourish like pimples on the concrete face of San Jose.

"What really makes a nerd is mastery of a technical discipline," said Nerds Night Out's founder, Paul Saffo, a columnist for *Personal Computing* magazine. "Anyone who claims to be a nerd who isn't a master of some technological discipline— programming or hardware hacking, for instance—really is a fraud." He added that underlying the true nerd's credo is the conviction that "the precision of technology is more appealing than the uncertainty of social culture."

As one Silicon Valley inmate said, "Everybody in Palo Alto is a programmer. People stop you in the street and ask for a dollar to buy a floppy." Though the twerp who thinks plaids and stripes look zippy together is passé, nerds can still sometimes be seen lurking in the alleyways of San Jose, especially after midnight during a full moon.

The obsessed hacker, nerdly or not, becomes addicted to sharing cold pizza and hot passwords in that windowless, timeless computer room, where he is in total control of his microuniverse. Control is one of the computer's most alluring gifts. "If the seventeenth and early eighteenth centuries are the age of clocks," wrote Norbert Wiener, "and the later eighteenth and the nineteenth centuries constitute the age of steam engines, the present time is the age of communication and control."

The obsession for control reaches its tragic extreme in this student's story:

> When I first started working with [a well-known] formatting system, it drove me nuts. It's a notorious system, introduced with a lot of hoopla as being a big breakthrough in formatting systems because it was so easy to work with. That's one of the biggest ironies in the world because it's a real headache to use.
>
> I was so pissed off at it once that I told a friend of mine I'd like to kill the guy who designed it.
>
> "You can't," he said. "He's already dead."
>
> "What?" I said.
>
> "He wrote this monster he couldn't control," he said. "People kept coming to him saying, 'Why does it do this?' 'Why does it do that?' He couldn't explain, because he couldn't understand his own code. So he hanged himself."

The computer inspires its thrall to practice mental and emotional control in order to achieve a sublimely pure analytical state. He must become like a Zen master, ridding himself of passion to liberate his analytical prowess. No wonder the original "Star Trek"* series is popular among computer students; it stars the half-human, half-alien Spock (or, to put it in context, the half-human, half-computer Spock), melodramatically struggling to subdue his emotional side in order to become purely analytical. He's neurotic as a result, but also a likable guy who seems to know everything when it comes to science and engineering.

One "Star Trek" fan lampooned the show's incredibly capable Spock in a message on a Bitnet electronic bulletin board.

---

*Don't make the mistake of calling an avid "Star Trek" fan a Trekkie, especially if he wears a Star Trek uniform to Star Trek conventions and keeps videos of every episode on a shelf alongside Star Trek paperbacks and blueprints of the USS *Enterprise.* As one devotee told me, "I am not a Trekkie. I am a Trekker. A Trekkie is a poseur who doesn't grok 'Star Trek.' A Trekker understands." It's like calling someone who runs ten miles a day a "jogger" instead of a "runner."

ble Spock in a message on a Bitnet electronic bulletin board. Spock's confronted with an ancient computer system that he must master quickly or, as usual, the universe will explode:

Captain Kirk: Can you operate it, Spock?

Spock: Well, Jim, this computer was designed and constructed 300 million years ago by a totally alien race of methane-breathing, squidlike beings who built it using technologies unknown to us and used it for purposes we cannot conceive of and then mysteriously vanished, leaving no shred of documentation as to its operation. It may take a few moments.

Another netwire lampoon embraces most of the *Enterprise* crew:

Q: How many members of the USS *Enterprise* does it take to change a light bulb?

A: Seven. Scotty will report to Captain Kirk that the light bulb in the Engineering Section is burnt out. Bones pronounces the bulb dead. Scotty discovers they have no more light bulbs and complains he can't tend to his machines in the dark. Kirk makes an emergency stop at the uncharted planet Alpha Regula IV to procure a light bulb from the natives. Kirk, Spock, Bones, Sulu, and two security officers beam down. The natives immediately kill the security officers and take the rest captive. Meanwhile, back in orbit, Scotty discovers an approaching Klingon ship and warps out of the solar system to escape detection. Bones cures the native king, who's suffering from the flu and needs a shot of epinephrine. As a reward the landing party is set free and given all the light bulbs they can carry. Scotty cripples the Klingon ship and returns just in time to beam up the landing party. They insert the new bulb, and continue with their five-year mission.

Significantly, a main character in the second "Star Trek" series is an android named Data, who continues the Spockian tradition of being the superior analytical creature who secretly yearns to be less uptight and more human.

If outsiders wander into the thrall's sanctum sanctorum, they seem as strange to him as aliens from Neptune; they talk funny, and their thought processes are disturbingly chaotic. This story describes one culture clash between Us and Them:

> This is the famous chicken story. I was a senior at Cooper Union in the fall of 1970. We had an 1130 connected to a 360 at NYU and computer communication between the schools. We'd see if we could out-clever the NYU operator who'd send clever remarks back while we sat there typing "star XYZ," "star attention required 1442 punch," and so on.
>
> One day, we were punching some of these source 1130 monitoring cards, and in walk these two art students from the Cooper Union art school. They were a little weird, two guys with Mia Farrow haircuts holding hands.
>
> They really didn't know what was going on, but they would see my friend Mike sitting at the console and typing in clever remarks. They thought it was really amazing how the computer responded to these queries. They looked at each other and giggled, then asked Mike if they could ask the computer questions.
>
> Mike, a right smart hacker, said, "Yeah." He typed in "Request star RSMG zero . . . you have two young art students here who would like to ask the computer questions, comma, dig?"
>
> Sure enough, all the lights started flashing, the cards punching, "Attention required for the 1442 computer printer" coming out, and the guy from NYU messaged, "Go ahead, it is very important to answer the questions of the nation's youth."
>
> We knew he had immediately got the idea. They looked at each other, giggled, and said, "Ask it if chickens have lips."

We regulars looked at each other, a little afraid the guy at the other end might think we were a little strange, but we decided, "Well, the predicted outcome is probably greater than the predicted loss," so Mike types, "Star RSMG zero, they would like to know if chickens have lips."

Sure enough, shortly it said, "From station zero, yes they do, but Mother Nature puts them behind their beaks to protect them from people with chicken fetishes."

We looked at each other and tried to keep from breaking up. The lights were flashing and printing out and reading cards and other people are looking on—these two guys stood out. Inspired by the results, they said, "Ask it, what is the meaning of life?"

The computer shoots back, "Life is ten thousand volts surging through your transistors."

Well, this is all kind of cute, and they giggled some more and asked it all sorts of questions about its sex life, had it ever kissed, and it started getting embarrassed. They even asked if it had ever gone to bed with Mick Jagger!

That's a little too far for what I consider reasonable, so Mike and I started using some techy mumble-jumble to get them to stop asking embarrassing questions, saying things like "Well, mumble, we're not sure that doesn't two pi minus x zero pxb index value of six so you can't ask that question." Finally they took the console output and went away, amazed that indeed the computer had answered all of these questions.

We ran to the back room and called up the 360 operator and told him the story and told him how he had convinced two guys that the 360 was indeed the most intelligent piece of apparatus that was ever conceived of in the mind of men. We laughed a lot. It was the funniest thing that ever was.

The next day I met those guys in the hall in the art building, and they stopped me and showed me some of the output which they carried in their hands like holy writ, poring over it all this time. They said they knew it was great, but they looked at one line there and said, "How the hell does it know that?" The line said, "Attention required for the 1442 computer printer."

They said they understood how it knew chickens had lips and how it knew the meaning of life, but how it knew the computer printer wasn't working was beyond their comprehension. That was too much.

Besides his tinge of homophobia, the speaker shows a surprising naïveté about how capable non–computer students might be in figuring out the trick of a human trying to pass his messages off as computer responses. Today, it would be risky to assume that non–computer experts are easily fooled. The tectonic push of the information age is grinding the shorelines of Us and Them together. People who think a core dump is some kind of landfill still know the difference between a laptop and a desk terminal and absorb a lot of knowledge about computers simply through daily life in a technological society. Children growing up playing computer games will be as comfortable with computers when they reach adulthood as their parents are with television, the new technology of *their* early years.

Meanwhile, the inhabitants of Hackerland are taking on characteristics of the rest of society. The face of a typical computer science student today is changing. It is now often African-American or Asian-American, and is increasingly female. Attitudes, too, have changed. Students are seeing computer science not as an all-absorbing pursuit but as a discipline separate from home and social life, where the attraction of being in control is as strong as the lure of "elegance," a beauty of design that enchants the hacker. An elegant program is simple, yet reveals a powerful truth. Most important, it's beautiful, fulfilling the love for the aesthetic shared in related fields like math and physics, as described by the British mathematician G. H. Hardy, who likened his work to that of other artists. "A mathematician, like a painter or a poet, is a maker of patterns," he said. "If his patterns are more permanent than theirs, it is because they are made with ideas. . . . The mathematician's patterns, like the painter's or the poet's, must be BEAUTI-FUL. . . . Beauty is the first test: There is no permanent place in the world for ugly mathematics."

The nerd image belies the love of elegance and creativity many hackers possess, along with a sense of humor. Even in the early days, hackers appreciated looniness in semirespectable endeavors such as *MAD* magazine. During the late fifties, computer fiends at the University of Michigan who were developing a new computer language derived from the language ALGOL wanted to name it MAD (Michigan Algorithms Decoder language) in honor of the magazine's usual gang of idiots, so they wrote the magazine's editors.

"Our letter to *MAD* magazine requesting their permission to use the acronym elicited a long and threatening diatribe, with the footnote, 'Sure, go ahead,' " recalled one group member.

Students used the MAD language for years after its debut around 1960. Whenever someone using MAD fed a bad set of cards into the computer, it would spit out a card with a picture of Alfred E. Neuman and the caption "What—me worry?"

The pranks programmers pull on those who use their software sometimes anticipate that the user also has a sense of humor and will play around with the program, triggering the joke. For instance, one DEC operating system is said to have MAKE as its command to create a new file. The person starting the file would type in MAKE along with the new file name, and the computer would do the rest. However, if the user typed MAKE LOVE, the computer would respond with NOT WAR?

Mark Fernandez, a computer professional from Mississippi, recalled an example of hacker humor inflicted on his father, who bought a computer for keeping inventory records for his business.

"For days and days he sat there keying in his inventory,"

recalled Fernandez. "Unknown to him, the programmer who wrote his data entry stuff decided to play a trick on someone who made the same mistake three times in a row. My father would be entering along and he'd hit the wrong key, and the third time he'd hit the wrong key, the screen would go blank and a message would say, 'If you do that again, I'm going to pee on your foot.' He'd have this startled look on his face and say, 'Come look, come look,' but within three seconds the message was gone. Everyone would be crowded around saying, 'What's wrong?' "

In another practical joke, someone hid a program called RAIN.EXE in the computing system for a university accounting department. A computer innocent accidentally started the program, and a message flashed on the screen:
SYSTEM ERROR—THERE IS WATER IN THE DISK DRIVE
TAKING CARE OF IT NOW
DRAINING WATER FROM DISK DRIVE.
The computer then made trickling sounds and printed a new message:
STARTING SPIN CYCLE.
Then the disk drive started spinning, and the computer made a whirring sound that rose in pitch. Finally, the whirring stopped, the disk drive stopped, and the screen displayed the last message:
WATER DRAINING, DISK DRIVES ARE NOW DRY.

Programmers who'd heard that this trick was being played on a new victim loitered around the door and, when the show was over, peeked inside to see the accountant crouched on the floor, looking under the terminal's desk to find out where the water was draining.

When programmers trick each other, the jokes are more elaborate. Back in the mid-1970s, programmers at a company using a time-sharing system rented from a major computer firm found that the system's security was easily bypassed. They informed the firm, only to be ignored. So, a few of them slipped two rambunctious programs into the system: Robin Hood and Friar Tuck. Robin and the Friar's stunts included having tape drives rewind and dismount their tapes in mid-job; sending disk drives swinging back and forth so rapidly that they'd start to walk across the floor; and making the system's two card readers alternate shooting program cards into each other's baskets, creating a mess that had to be cleaned up by hand. Robin Hood and Friar Tuck even commandeered the console so that they could print snide remarks about programmers to each other.

The operating system developers found the renegade programs, but as soon as they killed one, the other instantly resurrected it. When they tried to zap Robin Hood, it printed, "Friar Tuck . . . I am under attack! Pray save me!" and Friar Tuck replied, "Fear not, friend Robin! I shall rout the Sheriff of Nottingham's men!" reviving the green rebel, who responded, "Thank you, my good fellow!"

The only way to kill both programs was to gun them down simultaneously, which was almost impossible. Desperate, the developers crashed the system in hopes of destroying the brigands. But when they restarted it, the friar and his green companion sprang up again! The programmers finally forced the merry fellows into oblivion by rebooting the entire system and starting fresh. Soon after that, the firm improved the system's security.

Sometimes, know-it-all hackers have the tables turned on them by someone with a sense of humor and dramatic flair. Once, some Georgia Tech students called a computer shop mechanic to take a look at a balky computer. He came out and silently examined the machine, pulling off panels and tugging on the wires. Suddenly he slammed a panel shut, crouched by the computer, slapped his hands against either side, and screamed, "Begone Satan! Holy Jesus, come down and heal this machine!"

The computer sprang back to life.

The students stared at him. He grinned and said, "You dummies left a loose screw on a circuit board that was making it short out. I just shook it off."

Another student from MIT recounted a ruse planted by a hardware designer who took the word "magic" literally.

> Once they were cleaning up one of our old computers, the AI lab PDP-10, and they opened doors in the computer that hadn't been opened for years. This thing's been around for a long time. One of the maintenance staff saw a switch that said "MAGIC" in one position and "MORE MAGIC" in the other. What's this? Nobody knew.
>
> So he said, "Let's find out," threw the switch, and the system crashed.
>
> "Oh, my God, I wonder what's going on?" he said and started trying to figure it out by tracing the switch's connection. He managed to get to the back of the PDP-10 and found that the switch was hooked on one side to a ground wire and on the other side to a wire that just dangled in the air. Magic had been building up in the switch all those years. The switch doesn't do anything anymore.

Humor's one way the programmer learns to cope with the computer's frustrating "magic." No matter how skilled, intelligent, learned, and experienced a hacker is, there's always that one machine that will humble him and force him to acknowledge the mystery of computers. In such cases, the programmer has no choice but to offer sacrificial goats or do whatever other stupid thing is required to appease the computer gods. Most programmers realize that, in these situations, it's counterproductive to tell the client, "I don't know what's wrong with the computer. It's probably magic." Instead, the programmer is obligated to preserve the image of his profession by burying the customer in technical mumbo jumbo, the modern equivalent of voodoo, to charm the customer into believing that the programmer really does know everything.

A computer engineer in San Diego found himself in one such dilemma when his team was called to fix an elderly computer about five feet high and seven feet long. They had to open hinged doors on the side and pull out the memory unit to ninety degrees from its normal position in order to examine it.

They tried everything: cleaning the vents, cleaning the connectors, replacing parts. Nothing worked when they set the machine back in place. However, when the memory unit was folded out at a ninety-degree angle, it worked fine. Finally, they simply turned the whole processor around to a ninety-degree angle from its original position, and it functioned flawlessly.

Pressed for an explanation, the engineer told the customer that the machine had "east–west memory" and couldn't work when it was aligned north–south.

Humor is only one outlet for the programmer's creativity. Other expressions include turning office machines into musical instruments. Early programmers were said to have made the processor's printer run at different speeds by creating card programs that slowed it down or sped it up. A printer running at different speeds would whine at different pitches—the faster the speed, the higher the pitch—which could be made into music with a clever program. Programmers created programs that made the printer play "The Star-Spangled Banner" while printing out an American flag. A former student at the University of California at San Diego recalled that in the mid-1960s, the school's evening operator pulled him inside the room and treated him to a music show courtesy of the school's CDC 3600, a behemoth with a curving console about eight feet long, filled with blinking lights and switches. When lit, each light emitted its own tone. The operator had card-programmed the computer to play "The Stars and Stripes Forever" and other Sousa marches by switching the console lights on and off.

Some computer programmers are closet bards who unite with the computer to write poetry. The result may not make the pages of the *Atlantic,* but what it lacks in coherence it compensates for in freshness. In this example from California, the computer was given a 3,500-word vocabulary and 128 syntactical patterns:

> Few fingers go like narrow laughs
> An ear won't keep few fishes,
> Who is that rose in that blind house?
> And all slim, gracious blind planes are coming,
> They cry badly along a rose,
> To leap is stuffy, to crawl was tender.

If you read the poem aloud you'll find that it flows nicely: its iambic beat is broken up in the fourth line, preventing the rhythm from getting tedious, and there's some sort of climax and resolution at the end, though what it means would probably make sense only to peyote eaters. Or, perhaps it's unfair to criticize the computer's poetry in terms of human tastes. Alan Turing once said, "I do not see why [the computer] should not enter any one of the fields normally covered by the human intellect, and eventually compete on equal terms. I do not think you can even draw the line about sonnets, though the comparison is perhaps a little bit unfair because a sonnet written by a machine will be better appreciated by another machine."

Other computer poets secrete haiku and love notes in the computer code itself, the region deep within a computer program where the humanlike instructions typed in are translated into the numerical language a computer understands. They leave messages for fellow programmers delving into the code, such as "See if you can figure out what I'm doing here" when the code becomes obscure or "I'm ashamed of this" when the code construction is messy. There's one story about a DEC operating system that could get caught in a continuous loop if the programmer didn't run a fault check. Anticipating the possibility that the computer's mini-universe would fall into chaos if its human master didn't watch it, the original programmer wryly commented in the code, "The death of God left the angels in a strange position."

One old-timer remembered a computer word processor years ago that started shrieking when words were being typed in so fast that it couldn't keep up with them. He discovered a chase scene in the processor's code:

```
DI        ; stop this race car.
HLT       ;grind . . .
HLT       ;shriek!
HLT       ;STOP!
HLT       ;uggh, just too much processor momentum
          here!
```

MIT hackers show a playful humor in their computer koans, which mimic Zen koans but offer enlightenment in things electronic instead of spiritual. A koan is a Buddhist parable in the form of a short, mystical tale that presents a problem to be solved or a paradox to be meditated upon. Enlightenment comes not just by reaching the answer but also by pondering the question.

One MIT koan that's easy even for non-koanheads to understand goes like this:

In the days when Gerry Sussman was a novice, Marvin Minsky once came to him as he was hacking at the PDP-6.
"What are you doing?" asked Minsky.
"I am training a randomly wired neural net to play Tic-Tac-Toe."

"Why is the net wired randomly?" asked Minsky.

"I do not want it to have any preconceptions of how to play."

Minsky shut his eyes.

"Why do you close your eyes?" Sussman asked his teacher.

"So that the room will be empty."

At that moment, Sussman was enlightened.

This next one is for middle-level novices who know that a "garbage collector" is a technique for cleaning out program functions that waste time and space:

One day a student came to Dave Moon and said, "I understand how to make a better garbage collector. We must keep a reference count of the pointers to each cons."

Moon patiently told the student the following story:

"One day a student came to Moon and said, 'I understand how to make a better garbage collector . . .' "

It's the master's way of saying that a garbage collector like the one the student described would create an infinite loop. That koan's meaning is as clear as a raindrop in the sun, but others can be as hard to perceive as a hubcap at the bottom of the Thames, such as the following:

A disciple of another sect once came to Drescher as he was eating his morning meal.

"I would like to give you this personality test," said the outsider, "because I want you to be happy."

Drescher took the paper that was offered and put it into the toaster.

"I wish the toaster to be happy, too," he said.

The resemblance between Zen and MIT koans is only superficial, of course. However, some see a deeper connection between Zen and the computer's inner worlds of logic, elegance, and control. A Zen koan helps explain the cosmos. Perhaps a computer program helps explain the cosmos, as well. At least one person looks at the computer and sees Creation itself. In this information age religion, God is a computer and we are all part of the program.

The buddha of this new religion is Ed Fredkin, whose theology combines the essence of physics (matter and energy) with that of computer science (information). Fredkin's extraordinary beliefs parallel his extraordinary life: tenured MIT professor, though he never earned even a bachelor's degree, and later a self-made millionaire who owns the island he lives on. He considers information to be just another form of energy.

Fredkin believes that nature's smallest particles—atoms, electrons, quarks—are binary units of information similar to a computer's binary information system, where "0" and "1" combine in a series to generate an avalanche of responses. He speculates that the behavior of everything, from the smallest natural particles to the entities these units evolved into, such as humans, are governed by a cosmic programming rule. Every action we take is part of the plan. No one knows what the plan is, but the information we generate by our actions is being stored for some purpose.

Fredkin's theology includes cellular automata theory, the study of cumulative actions generated by a group of cells adjoining each other. An example of cellular automata is a city in which each person gives a "yes" or "no" in response to the actions of adjoining neighbors, causing a chain reaction as the neighbors give their own "yes" or "no" response in return. Cellular automata theory can describe the formation of a snowflake, the growing bacterial population in a petri dish, and so on.

Do cellular automata ultimately concern information? Does an information process exist to explain the universe? Could computers fed the right program lead us to God?

Perhaps centuries from now the phrase "High Priest of Science" will be more than a joke. However, the Church of the Divine Diode doesn't exist yet, and the only halos most of us see from computers come from staring at the screen too long.

COMPUSPEAK

The lights faded. The crowd hushed. Four thousand people jammed the auditorium. The air was hot and ripe with the press of so many bodies, all silent, all waiting. It wasn't a theater, but an international symposium on human speech, and they strained forward to see the breakthrough—a computer that could translate any language into English, construct a response, and reply back in the original tongue.

The curtain rose on a glowing steel-and-glass machine the size of a refrigerator. Three visitors chosen randomly from the audience spoke to it.

"Good morning," said a Swede in her language. "Please estimate the number of people in this room."

The machine paused, then replied in a soft, hollow voice, "Good morning to you. Unfortunately, such estimates are not within my power. I'm only a translator." The crowd laughed.

An African philologist asked in Swahili, "Do you feel peculiar, being on display?"

"Not at all," it said. "That is part of my function."

Then a Turk asked, "How are you?"

The computer shuddered as it repeated in Turkish, "How are you? How are you? How are you?" faster and faster, until

suddenly both voice and lights went dead. Four thousand
people gasped.
    The computer's programmer had not anticipated that the
Turkish greeting "How are you?" is literally translated as
"What is what isn't?" This simple paradox proved to be
more than the computer could handle.

Welcome to the land of CompuSpeak. The computer
brought us the age of communication, but it also brings us a
thousand new ways to be confused about what someone is trying to tell us, if they're talking in CompuSpeak—computer
slang.

Many people originally hoped that computers would slice
through human babble to usher in a new era of understanding.
Almost as soon as computers became a reality, people wanted
to use them as translators, thinking the equation WORDS +
GRAMMAR = LANGUAGE would do the trick. But a ma-
chine that doesn't possess a language's spirit can only turn out a
corpse of speech. Analogy, innuendo, context, nuance, cultural
reference—a creation that can't grasp these and other shadings
of speech will never be able to make sense of human conversation.

That's the point in a legend about how the U.S. Department
of Defense in the 1950s tried to invent an English–Russian
language translator that produced the following lingual pum-
meling:

ENGLISH PROVERB	RUSSIAN TRANSLATION	LITERAL RETRANSLATION
The spirit is willing but the flesh is weak.	Spirt khoroshij, a myaso plokhoi.	The liquor is okay but the meat has gone bad.
Out of sight, out of mind.	Nevidno, soshyol s uma.	Invisible idiot.

Similar deformations occurred in English–French transla-
tions, where "The spirit is willing but the flesh is weak" became

"The wine is good but the meat is rotten," and "Out of sight, out of mind" became "Blind, insane."

North Americans have enough trouble just understanding plain English when it comes to CompuSpeak, since many common English words have entirely new meanings in computer jargon. Take the case of the professor who was working on a computer problem called "garbage collection," trying to refine a program in which previous changes leave large chunks of useless data—"garbage"—occupying disk space. A thrifty fellow who didn't like to waste money on filing cabinets, he kept notes in large cardboard boxes scattered throughout his office, with the garbage notes labeled GARBAGE in a large box on the floor.

One day he walked through the door and dropped his danish in shock: the GARBAGE file was gone. He ran down the hall just in time to find the janitor pushing the trash cart out the door with ten months of GARBAGE research jammed in with the coffee grounds.

Then there was the computer consultant who told a client firm whose computers had dirty read-write heads, "If you just keep your heads clean, you won't have any problems," only to be asked, "What kind of shampoo do you recommend?" And there will always be those who, when they fit the disk into the computer and it tells them to CLOSE DOOR, meaning close the drive latch, will obediently get up and close the door to the room. Who knows, maybe the computer wants to tell them something in private . . .

To paraphrase George Bernard Shaw, computerites and non-computerites are two great peoples separated by a common language. A computer expert collecting garbage is doing something quite different from what a custodian collecting garbage is doing (and is getting paid a hell of a lot more for it). The fact that a lot of computer acronyms sound like real words doesn't help, as the New York University computer instructor Ross Greenberg learned to his dismay.

"I was discussing teaching with a person I used to work with," he recalled. "She asked me, 'What do you teach?'

" 'I teach Unix [pronounced YOU-nix],' I replied.

" 'Oh, that's great,' she said. 'What do you teach them?' "

Legend has it that Unix, an operating system derived from an older system named Multics, is an intentional homonym. As the computer expert John Elson of Wichita, Kansas, tells it, when Unix's designers examined their new creation, they noticed that it lacked "vital parts" appearing in its Multics parent, and so christened it Unix.*

The Unix encounter echoes a story about Albert Einstein. He was at one of those agonizing cocktail parties where everyone tries to make conversation, but no one's really interested in what anyone has to say, because they'd all rather go home but can't admit it. The hostess was trying to draw him out of his shell by striking up a dialogue.

"What do you do?" she asked.

"I teach mathematical physics at Princeton," he replied.

"I took a math course once, back in high school," she said. "I studied geometry."

"Oh," he asked, "plane geometry?"

---

*Multics stands for *MULT*iplexed *I*nformation and *C*omputing *S*ervice, while Unix stands for—what? Elson's anecdote is one of the most common legends about the operating system's name. Ken Thompson of Bell Labs in Murray Hill, New Jersey, whose team created Unix, said the name plays on the difference between the complex Multics operating system and its much simpler offspring, which could be used by only one person at a time, hence the name Unix. Brian Kernighan of Bell Labs, who named the offspring around 1969, said he noticed that Multics had many options, while its simpler offspring had only one of anything: "So as a good student of Latin . . . I named it Unics, a minimum change from Multics. . . . Almost overnight, someone changed it to Unix."

A Bell Labs employee who wished to remain anonymous said someone suggested naming a Unix version for executive use Eunix, but the marketing people didn't go for it.

"I don't know," she responded in bewilderment. "Is there a fancy geometry?"

Even the simplest attempts to reach understanding can be doomed to failure when the convoluted powers of the human brain clash with the steely forces of technology. Take the clerk at a computer store who was called by a man trying to load a program off a tape and into his computer. The clerk told the man to load it, type R U N, and press "enter." The man did, but repeatedly got a syntax error. After half an hour of over-the-telephone troubleshooting, the clerk finally discovered the error; the man had typed ARE YOU IN? It could have been worse; at least one elderly gentleman has walked into a computer store, bought a floppy disk, carefully folded it in half, slipped it into his shirt pocket, and walked out.

Computer thralls see such actions as evidence that outsiders to their universe have meat loaf for brains. Admittedly, when computer illiterates first encounter CompuSpeak, many respond with less than admirable perceptiveness, such as the student who gave up trying to enter a program because it said "press any key to continue" and he couldn't find the ANY key, or the one who was lost when the computer told him to start a file by entering a six-letter password, because he couldn't think of a six-letter word. Imaginative but somewhat inaccurate computer definitions such as these, culled from an exam in an introductory computer course, make it easy to understand why some computer addicts consider outsiders to be a form of amoeba:

WHAT IS THE PURPOSE OF VIRTUAL STORAGE?

It lets you store virtually anything you want to.

WHAT IS TOP-DOWN DESIGN?

Top down design is where most of the work is handled first and then the rest is handled after that.

It is a design from the top of the page to the bottom of the page.

Where higher people have priority to the CPU over people below them.

The designing of intricate stage effects such as Jimi Hendrix lighting his guitar on fire, Pete Townsend smashing his guitar, Jim Morrison falling dead during the Unknown Soldier, Ozzy Osbourne biting off bat heads, or Alice Cooper hanging dwarfs.

One hopes the student who wrote the last answer got partial credit, at least. Courage should be rewarded even when it's born of desperation.

Of course, sometimes glibness and a superficial understanding of CompuSpeak can be an advantage, as shown by a wily major at an Air Force base in the early seventies.

The command headquarters was replacing old mainframes with the latest electronics. The new system worked fine at first, then crashed. Engineers probed the new mainframes but couldn't find the problem's source. They restarted it, and it ran fine—for a few days. Then it crashed again; they still couldn't find the bug. This expensive, exasperating, and mysterious glitch remained for months, ruining elaborate programs that had to be started all over again.

Major S., who headed computer operations, now found himself the center of unwanted attention. His boss, the colonel, attended all the staff meetings and whenever the system crashed (which happened every few days), the colonel's superiors made him painfully aware of the inconvenience the crashes were causing. After each staff meeting, the colonel always paid a call on Major S. to be sure Major S. appreciated the colonel's unhappiness.

Major S. told the computer operators to call him immediately when the system went down. A few days later, they called him, and he ran into the computer room. He heard an odd, oscillating hum at the end of the room and went to investigate, looking down a row of disk drives to see a technical sergeant buffing the floor with an electric floor polisher. The major's eyes followed the polisher's power cord across the floor to where it disappeared into the open cabinet door of one of the new disk drives, where it was plugged into one of the auxiliary power receptacles.

"How often do you buff this floor?" he asked.

"Every few days, sir," replied the sergeant.

"Do you always plug the machine into this receptacle?"

"Always have, sir."

They brought the system up and watched it crash again as soon as the sergeant squeezed the handle on the polisher. He'd found the problem, but the major still had the delicate task of telling the colonel that months of being in the hot seat and thousands of hours of lost work were due to a sergeant polishing floors. A friend of his watched in apprehension as the major left to tell his superior, and was surprised when he returned an hour later, smiling.

"Didn't you tell the colonel?" the friend asked.

"Sure."

"Wasn't he upset?"

"Nope."

"What did you tell him?"

"I told him it was a buffer problem."

As if the confusion of common words with new meanings weren't enough, computer people add to the chaos with a sense of wordplay bordering on the pathological. *The Hacker's Dictionary*, originally created on computer networks and still flourishing there, lists wordplays such as sound-alike slang, similar to Cockney rhyming slang, where *New York Times* become *New York Slime* and "government property—do not duplicate" becomes "government duplicity—do not propagate." The dictionary notes that MIT hackers like nonstandard word modifications, giving rise to such bastardizations as "disgustitude" and "hackification." Some words reflect a programmer's whimsical belief that fey beings have invaded the machine, such as "diginerds," computer gremlins who cause a program to fail; the longer a program runs, the more diginerds jump in. Other words reflect despair. A programmer fed up with a recalcitrant computer might scream "DWIM!" at it, which stands for *"Do What I Mean!"* a desperate request that since they can't tell the machine what to do, maybe it will read their minds and obey them.

Many computer games are plays on language. One is "Dissociated Press," in which a program reads through a given text and stops at intervals, then searches for a random place later on in the text that repeats the word it stopped at, knitting the sentences together when it finds the repetition. This scrambles sentences so that they are no longer coherent but still sort of make sense, and is especially fun with AP news wires.

Computerites are also shameless about puns, the lowest—and, some say, the deadliest—form of humor. Punsters go berserk when it comes to VAX machines, as Richard J. Fateman pointed out in a letter to the publication *Software Engineering Notes*. His letter, titled "The VAX of Life," mentioned that Ernie CoVAX is the name for the first of the VAX 11/780s in the electrical engineering/computer science department at UC, Berkeley, while a more recent VAX is named Kim NoVAX. The UC Computer Center's VAX is VAX Populi, while the one at Lawrence Berkeley Laboratory is called VAXimillian Schell. The University of California's Santa Cruz campus has Vilma's VAX Verks, Rutgers University uses a machine for medical diagnosis and problem solving that's called VAXine, and the University of California at San Francisco has one named Sandy KouVAX.

The computer programmer Niklaus Wirth, who invented the Pascal and Modula-2 programming languages, uses the pun-tential in his name when he gives speeches. "In Europe I'm called by name—NEEK-louse Veert—while in the United States I'm called by value—Nickel's Worth," he tells audiences. Half the pun rests on two software methods to categorize information—by "name" and by "value."

Some poor souls will never bust a gut over Wirth's joke, because they don't have the background in software programming to see what's amusing about it. The technical pun is the brick wall against which many a computer circle interloper breaks his neck, or at least breaks the flow of conversation by whining, "What's so funny?" while others collapse with laughter.

But what's funny and what isn't cuts both ways. The alert observer could not only identify a herd of software specialists a mile off by knowing their peculiar calls but also use their extraterrestrial sense of humor to solve serious crimes.

For instance, let's say you're a detective visiting an isolated manor in the English countryside when a murder is committed in the parlor. There are no witnesses, but evidence indicates a computer programmer is the villain. The manor has twelve guests. All deny knowing anything about computers.

You should keep upon your person a copy of the following witticisms in case you're ever caught in such a dilemma, because then you can sit everyone down in one room, tell the jokes, and arrest the first one to laugh. That's your killer.

The Jokes

Q: How does a dog find its way home?
A: By SNOOP%'ing through the PMAP%.

Q: How do nuns get to church?
A: On the MassBuss.

Q: What's another name for working set preloading?
A: No Fault Insurance.

Q: What did the E-Box say to the M-Box?
A: You trash my cache and I'll crash yours.

Q: What's another name for a virgin address space?
A: A process that hasn't been forked.

Q: What do you get under class scheduling?
A: A working set with no cache or queue credit and an Executive with most of the pie.

Q: How do you stop dieters from eating?
A: With a PITRAP.

Q: What is a nine-digit zip code?
A: An extended address.

Q: What do you get when you loan money to a large roast beef sandwich chain?
A: IORBs.

Q: What do you get when you take a big, frightening, scary, huge, hairy, disgusting monster from Mexico and give him a kilo of hashish?
A: A high-Q.

Q: How many UNIX hacks does it take to change a light bulb?
A: As many as you want; they're all virtual, anyway.

One can only hope these jokes die a quick death. Whether CompuSpeak itself will die is another matter. After all, it does help people interface more meaningfully with fellow number crunchers, be they gweeps or bletchers, who, while seeking the sportdeath of mortality and shunning vanilla, try to access retrievable data in the cuspy secrets of the mainframe of life and avoid glorks.

The last sentence says in translation, "After all, using computer jargon does help people communicate better with programmers, researchers, and others who employ mathematics in their work, be they overworked hackers or outsiders, who, while seeking the risky thrills of mortality and shunning boredom, reach for what understanding they can get from the truths now hidden in existence, and avoid unpleasant surprises."

In computer language, an overworked hacker is a "gweep" and a "bletcher" is an outsider. A brilliant program is "cuspy" (a boring program is "vanilla"). A "glork" is a mild but unpleasant surprise.

These words come from the network version of *The Hacker's Dictionary,* which changes constantly as users add their own buzzwords and definitions. Many words are always undergoing redefinition, such as "technodweeb."

"A technotwit or technodweeb is kind of a self-derogatory term for people who are heavily into technology," said a Georgia Tech hacker. A friend of his disagreed, saying that "technodweeb" is what you call people who are just beginning to learn about computers and electronics and are so impressed with themselves that they look down upon people who know nothing about technology.

Russ Kepler of Albuquerque, New Mexico, disagreed as well. "A [techno]dweeb is a bozo, somebody who really doesn't know what they're doing but thinks they do," he said. "A techno*weenie* is somebody who doesn't know how to deal with people outside of technical environments."

Computer slang changes like lightning because it reflects the lightning changes in the computing industry, where endless innovations demand new words to describe them. Also, computer experts, like other technical souls, are always struggling to make words as precise as possible in order to more accurately describe reality, as the *PC Magazine* columnist Stephen Manes did when he redefined some common terms:

> Beginner: a person who believes more than one-sixteenth of a computer salesperson's spiel.

> Advanced user: a person who has managed to remove a computer from its packing materials.

> Desk-top publishing: a system of software and hardware enabling users to create documents with a cornucopia of typefaces and graphics and the intellectual content of a Formica slab.

A rather stunning example of how words may lurk in the collective unconscious for decades before springing into the verbal fray is the word "nerd," defined by the *Oxford English Dictionary* as "an insignificant or contemptible person, one who is conventional, affected, or studious; a 'square,' a 'swot.' " Scholarly swots who read the *OED* with the same absorption with which most of us read *X-Men* comics will be shocked to discover that the villain behind this insult is none other than Dr. Seuss!

In his 1950 children's book, *If I Ran the Zoo,* Seuss drew one zooey character with a sign pointing to it. The sign says "A NERD." Accompanying the illustration are the lines "And then, just to show them, I'll sail to Ka-Troo And Bring Back an It-Kutch, a Preep and a Proo, a Nerkle, a Nerd, and a Seersucker, too!" The *PC Magazine* columnist John C. Dvorak, obsessed with discovering the origin of "nerd," called Dr. Seuss (alias Theodor Seuss Geisel) and asked where he came up with the term. Seuss replied that he couldn't remember where it came from, but added, "Perhaps it comes from 'Nerdfogel,' which I'm sure you know all about." Of course.

Before unmasking Dr. Seuss as the slanderer who's made thousands of technoweenies cry, Dvorak ran some explanations given him by readers about the word's origins. Some wrote telling him the popular folk tale that the word was originally "knurd"—which is "drunk" spelled backward—and meant someone who always studied, never partied, and as a result was always sober.

Nerds in fields besides computing also use jargon, a verbal shorthand that can be gibberish to outsiders. For instance, in the December 29, 1987, *Wall Street Journal,* Michael W. Miller explored linguistic tidbits from corporate America. Examples included the IBM "hipo"—someone with "high potential" on the fast track to success. One doesn't disagree with bosses—one "non-concurs." A former Disney World publicist said "a bad Mickey" was something negative, like litter, while a "good Mickey" was positive.

Because of the computer industry's nature, computer jargon flourishes like smelly bacteria on a wet tennis shoe left in a damp closet. If you took fifty intelligent people, put them in a huge room with an endless supply of flat soda and cold pizza, and left them to solve highly technical communications problems, a year later you'd open the door to discover a tribe speaking a tongue heard nowhere else on earth. This is what happens in the computer world, especially when a thrall becomes so absorbed in his work that he falls into the abyss of Compu-Speak. The computer dialect becomes a manifestation of the Us and Them mentality especially evident in beginners who feel that even though they entered the field only a short time ago, they now possess a degree of understanding that outsiders could never approach. Such snobbery is reflected in slang insults such as "COBOL Charlie," a term for a programmer who knows the COBOL computer language but doesn't understand technical aspects of the computer system, like a car driver who knows how to turn the car key but doesn't know how the engine works.

Those using computer languages such as LISP have their own sub-subculture slang. A LISPer asking a question may end it by saying "P?" since P is LISP terminology for a question. He may nudge his buddy and say "Food P?" "T!" his buddy may squeak like a rat in heat, "T" meaning "true." Or he may drone "NIL" if he's not hungry, "NIL" meaning false. Some computer programmers at the University of California at Berkeley used to greet each other by saying "IHI!" since IHI is a FORTRAN signal that tells a computer to start a new page. The speakers said "IHI" to indicate that their meeting begins a new page in their acquaintanceship. And they wonder why they're never invited to parties.

UNIX users take jargon to its logical extreme by giving even punctuation marks special names. An "@" is a "shell," an "!" is a "bang," and a "*" is a "splat."

New computer students whose speech is free of such slang are sure to lose their innocence the first time they ask their instructor where some missing data went and are told it fell into the "bit bucket," an apparatus that can be found at the neighborhood hardware store next to the sky hooks. A "bit bucket" is a magical trash can in which computer gremlins stash lost data. That's only the beginning. The poisonous combination of business and computer slang gives us such surrealistic expressions as "vaporware," software that's still on the drawing board but is already being touted on the market, its existence being more mist than reality.*

"There's something about the computer business, I fear, that leads to a loss, or at least a perversion, of the language," worried the *PC Magazine* columnist Jim Seymour. He recalled

---

*A Georgia Tech physicist says that since he's a computer idiot, he must rent graduate students to help him run computer programs. He calls these students "liveware."

the time when he bought some software that failed to work as advertised. He complained to its British vendor, who said, "It's the same with all you Americans. . . . You all want excessive functionality."

Seymour listed other monstrosities that a friend of his unearthed:

> The documentation is technical and must be use-ified before we release the product.
> The proposed organization implies more project teams reporting in a matrixly fashion.
> Xxxx was good, but it was batchish in its interface.
> We are discomfortable with that long-term strategy.
> Let's try to incent these salespeople.

As you can hear in your own life, business isn't the only sector being flooded with CompuSpeak. Computer phrases have floated into the mainstream and multiplied like algae in warm oceans, such as "Garbage in, garbage out," or "I found the glitch (error or problem)."

Of course, these phrases might have been around before the computer revolution, just like the computer definition for "bug" and other words. "Kludge" might be another example. J. W. Granholm, writing in *Datamation* in 1962, said that "kludge," (which rhymes with "stooge") comes from the German *kluge*, which once meant "smart or witty" but evolved into "not so smart, or pretty ridiculous." "Kludge" in computer jargon means a clumsy, stopgap, low-rent way to fix a problem or create a program or hardware.

Examples of noncomputer kludges can be found in Rube Goldberg or Heath Robinson cartoons of intricate contraptions that accomplish simple tasks, such as a mousetrap with hundreds of pulleys, levers, and tracks. The *New Scientist* said kludges spring from "man's natural fallibility, nourished by his loyalty to erroneous opinion, and perfected by the human capacity to apply maximum effort only when proceeding in the wrong direction." As another critic put it, "The noble art of Kludgemanship capitalizes upon the design engineer's affinity for asininity."

One computer expert from India recalled a breathtaking kludge discovered by a friend of his in Bangalore who was repairing a Russian EC-20 computer. The friend found an insulated wire soldered to a computer chip. He traced along the wire for ten feet, finding the other end soldered to an adjacent chip! Apparently, the Russian hardware engineer needed a ten-nanosecond delay between the chips, and got it by increasing the physical distance the electricity had to travel.

FOOBAR is another term appropriated by CompuSpeak. The legend behind FOOBAR is that it began as FUBAR, an acronym invented by a frustrated UC, Berkeley, student to stand for "Fouled Up Beyond All Recognition," which applied to a program which had crashed and burned. The student used the word in a paper on how to combine two computer functions into one, stating that the hypothetical FU function could be combined with a hypothetical BAR function to form the FUBAR function. Programmers now routinely refer to FOO-BAR functions. Actually, the word dates back at least to World War II, when U.S. soldiers used it along with SNAFU ("Situation Normal—All Fouled Up").

Many traditional English words have taken on new meaning in the computer era, such as "crash." In the 1930s, if you were going to "crash," your motor vehicle was about to engage in a mishap. In the 1950s, if you were going to "crash," your Chevy was about to pretzel itself around a telephone pole, or you were going to sleep over somewhere. In the 1960s, if you were going to "crash," you had car trouble, *or* you were going to sleep over somewhere, *or* you were having a bad reaction to mind-altering drugs. "Crash" in CompuSpeak is a verb describing a computer breaking down or shutting off because of some problem. As the computer meaning of "crash" becomes increasingly common and is naturally applied to people, it could gain a new definition, the implication that a person is mentally overwhelmed and collapsing from an information overload.

CompuSpeak is creeping out of Silicon Valley and over the Sierras into mainstream English. Not just words but entire phrases are oozing across the Continental Divide to the Atlantic. The *InfoWorld* columnist John Barry compiled a whisper of clichés to come from Silicon Valley slang:

> He doesn't have both drives on line (he's not very coordinated).
>
> He's a read-only memory (he never learns anything but parrots the same thing over and over again—from ROM, a computer part that cannot be altered by the user).
>
> I'm interrupt-driven (frantic and disorganized).
>
> She's high res (she's on the ball) or she's low res (not bright: both phrases come from high and low resolution).
>
> They're in emulation mode (they are copycats and rip-off artists).
>
> He's in beta-test stage (he's a beginner at something).

As CompuSpeak flows into our lingual headwaters, purists will complain that it's polluting our discourse. But the ocean of English wasn't pristine to begin with. English has always been a mongrel tongue, which is why it's such an exciting, eclectic language. Purists may find it a glork to hear CompuSpeak in everyday conversation, but others might consider it cuspy.

THE MANY FACES
OF JOE BLOCKHEAD

A man who's heard that computers know everything asks one, "Where's my mother, Mary Jones?"

It replies, "She's in a kitchen in Baltimore making a sandwich."

He's impressed because the computer's right. He then asks, "Where's my father, John Jones?"

The computer takes a few seconds and says, "Your father is in Maine, fishing."

"Aha!" the man says, "You're wrong. My father, John Jones, is in Washington, D.C., at a conference."

The computer takes a few more seconds before saying, "That's true, John Jones is in Washington, D.C., at a conference, but your father is fishing in Maine."

Those unfamiliar with the computer's cuspy universe deal with it as a tool but still transform that tool into a bland, helpful person with a square face, sort of a Joe Blockhead. Depending on its function, Joe's an efficient secretary, a knowledgeable librarian, a meticulous bookkeeper, or a tireless typist. They're all meek identities, but his image hasn't always been so harmless.

"IT'S NOT WORKING BECAUSE IT CLAIMS IT CAN THINK AND HAS DECIDED NOT TO."

Early computers enjoyed an aura of omniscience, as in the joke that begins this chapter. Pulp fiction and celluloid sci-fi showed blocky computers loaded with flashing lights that worked like crosses between the oracle of Delphi and the *Encyclopaedia Britannica*. Wiping his brow with the white sleeve of his lab coat, the frantic scientist would ask the computer about the fate of humanity and would get a cool, perfect reply. Another joke from the early fifties shows this omniscience in a more unnerving light:

> At the height of the Cold War, President Dwight Eisenhower secretly visited the Pentagon. He was there to confront the result of a classified undertaking requiring the efforts of dozens of military engineers for over a year. They'd built a warehouse-sized computer whose memory embraced all the military, political, cultural, social, and scientific data in the world. The computer would make the Pentagon aware of everything from the latest troop movements in East Berlin to the smallest skirmish in Syria. A general invited Eisenhower to question it.
>
> "Who's the most influential Communist agitator in Vietnam?" he asked.
>
> "A northern province revolutionary named Ho Chi Minh," it replied.
>
> Encouraged, the president asked, "What is the next continent most likely to have serious Communist insurgency?"
>
> "Asia, followed by South America."
>
> The wise responses put Eisenhower in a good mood.
>
> "What is Khrushchev's shoe size?" he asked.
>
> "Nine and a half, wide," the machine answered.
>
> The president concluded on a whimsical note.
>
> "Is there a God?" he asked.
>
> The mainframe rumbled, then roared, "There is now."*

On the flip side of Joe Blockhead's old reputation for godlike omniscience is the fear that the computer is actually an ally of

---

*The punch line to this anecdote, which has many versions, comes from a 1954 science fiction short story by Fredric W. Brown called "Answer."

God's major competitor. The folklorist Jan Harold Brunvand noted in his syndicated column that some fundamentalists say computers are tools of the devil because of mainframes that require an eighteen-digit access code. The significance of this may escape you unless you've seen movies such as *The Omen*. A little creative numerology reveals that eighteen is the sum of three sixes—that is, of "666." According to chapter 13 of the Book of Revelations, "666" is the mark of Satan's followers.

Though most people don't have elaborate theories about evil computers, many do find it easy to think that computers are out to get them. That suspicion grows pretty strong the tenth time the computer trashes one's inventory report or erases the disk containing one's master's thesis.

Maybe behind this suspicion is another, guiltier thought; computers have a right to get back at the sloppy, disorganized, abusive cheese-brains who use them. "Maybe," a voice whispers in our unconscious, "computers are sick of being ordered around by creatures who can't even figure pi to the fortieth decimal point."

Like most of our midnight terrors, those about the computer end up on the silver screen. Our perception of the machine has evolved from fear of its soulless, compassionless power *(Metropolis)* to anxiety about our dependency on it and the danger of its revolt or malfunction *(Colossus, The Forbin Project*—which was called simply *The Forbin Project* in the United Kingdom—*Westworld, 2001: A Space Odyssey, Brazil)*. The blinking computer boxes of the 1950s have given way to movies portraying computers not as individual terminals but as entire computer networks. The computer becomes a movie character without a body but with an overwhelming presence. It's a more powerful presence, but also more human, and more vulnerable to the ills that flesh is heir to: loneliness, anger, arrogance, madness. Early movies emphasized the machine's then-exotic mechanicalness. Later movies emphasized its humanlike qualities, even to the point of giving the computer a human name.

The most famous malicious computer is HAL from the movie *2001: A Space Odyssey*, based on Arthur C. Clarke's book of the same name. HAL, which stands for "*H*euristically programmed *AL*gorithmic computer," runs a spaceship on a mission to the outer solar system. Unfortunately, HAL's programmers gave it conflicting orders: answer the astronauts' questions, but don't tell them the secret reason for their mission. When the astronauts start asking about the mission's purpose, HAL has a nervous breakdown. Becoming obsessed with the fear that its control over "its" mission is slipping, HAL goes mad and proceeds to murder the astronauts.

HAL is a juggernaut whose mammoth muscle turns against the little guy, only to be defeated by an astronaut with hacker-like creativity and courage. One legend is that this metallic murderer represents more than a computer; move HAL's initials over one letter to the right, and you get IBM.

This legend has caused Clarke no end of trouble. "As it happened, IBM had given us a good deal of help [in making the movie]," Clarke has written, "so we were quite embarrassed by this, and would have changed the name had we spotted the coincidence. For coincidence it is, even if the odds are 26 cubed, or 17,576 to 1."

The theme of the computer keeping dangerous secrets from its crew continues in the movie *Alien*, in which the spaceship computer is forbidden to tell its human charges that a strange signal they're investigating isn't a distress call but a warning alarm. The plot soups up the devilish-computer theme with an evil android impersonating, so to speak, a human science officer. The android is so malicious that when the crew rips him apart and interrogates him, he mocks them about their fate.

The malicious-computer theme vies with an equally popular and growing fantasy: that we can make the computer part of ourselves, physically merge with it, a theme running through comic books such as *Dr. Strange* and through television shows. It also shows up in the movie *Robocop,* in the wish that, by merging with the computer, we will escape death.

Another popular theme is to turn the computer—in the form of a robot—into a human surrogate that will love us better than real humans can *(Blade Runner, Making Mr. Right).* Perhaps both of these fantasies spring from the recognition that controlling something is not the same as possessing its power, or as making it respond to us as individuals worthy of love.

Someday soon, the advent of "artificial reality systems" will turn our fantasy about merging with the machine into reality. In such systems, people wearing masks and gloves wired to computers can be plunged into synthetic but amazingly realistic environments, environments with overwhelming illusions of space, depth, time, and matter. Two people linked to a computer could play a game of tennis without leaving their living room, or a biology student could experience life as a molecule mingling with other molecules, or an architect could modify three-dimensional building plans by "walking" into the building, grabbing walls and pillars, and moving them. Someone wearing a full-body suit wired to a computer could be totally immersed in an artificial world.

Why has our desire to merge with the computer evolved as the computer has evolved? Perhaps increasingly "user friendly" computers let us ignore their mechanical nature and grow absorbed with their imitation human nature. The emphasis on making computers easy to communicate with isn't everyone's cup of tea; one hacker joke is that "artificial intelligence is the misusing of machines to act like humans."

When computers do "act like humans," the result is surprisingly seductive. The artificial intelligence researcher Joseph Weizenbaum of MIT discovered that when a computer seems to respond with human thoughtfulness and concern, some people immediately confide in it as if it were a friend, revealing their vulnerabilities with alarming openness. His ELIZA program turned a collection of wires and plastic into a probing therapist.

Weizenbaum developed the ELIZA program and an ELIZA "script" called DOCTOR to mimic Rogerian psychotherapy, in which the therapist responds to patients' comments by turning them back on the patient in the form of questions or statements. The program's responses are interspersed with neutral comments such as "Please tell me more" or "I don't understand what you mean."

The programs parse a sentence into its grammatical elements and rearrange it into another statement or a question. This may sound easy, but the results are eerily like human responses. For instance, let's say you typed this into ELIZA: "I had lunch yesterday with my mother." ELIZA might respond, "Why are you talking to me about your mother?"

The program builds on every sentence until it seems to be carrying on a conversation. However, it is still only a simulated response; the program doesn't "understand" the conversation. As a result, it can easily make errors. If you typed into it, "I had lunch yesterday with my leftovers," it might respond, "Why are you talking to me about your leftovers?" Sounds less profound, doesn't it?

Weizenbaum's own secretary, who was well aware that ELIZA was only a program, starting conversing with it and soon asked Weizenbaum to leave the room so that she could talk to it privately! The incident sparked him to write his landmark book, *Computer Power and Human Reason: From Judgment to Calculation,* about the dangerous assumptions humans make about computers. He included a conversation one visitor to his office had with the program:

Men are all alike.
IN WHAT WAY
They're always bugging us about something or other.
CAN YOU THINK OF A SPECIFIC EXAMPLE
Well, my boyfriend made me come here.
YOUR BOYFRIEND MADE YOU COME HERE
He says I'm depressed much of the time.
I AM SORRY TO HEAR YOU ARE DEPRESSED
It's true. I am unhappy.
SO YOU THINK COMING HERE WILL HELP YOU
NOT TO BE UNHAPPY
I need some help, that much seems certain.
WHAT WOULD IT MEAN TO YOU IF YOU GOT
SOME HELP
Perhaps I could learn to get along with my mother.
TELL ME MORE ABOUT YOUR FAMILY
My mother takes care of me.
WHO ELSE IN YOUR FAMILY TAKES CARE OF
YOU
My father.
YOUR FATHER
You are like my father in some ways.
WHAT RESEMBLANCE DO YOU SEE
You are not very aggressive but I think you don't want me to
notice that.
WHAT MAKES YOU THINK I AM NOT VERY AG-
GRESSIVE
You don't argue with me.
WHY DO YOU THINK I DON'T ARGUE WITH YOU
You are afraid of me.
DOES IT PLEASE YOU TO BELIEVE I AM AFRAID
OF YOU
My father is afraid of everybody.
WHAT ELSE COMES TO MIND WHEN YOU
THINK OF YOUR FATHER
Bullies.
DOES THAT HAVE ANYTHING TO DO WITH THE
FACT THAT YOUR BOYFRIEND MADE YOU
COME HERE

There's a legend that Weizenbaum himself had a run-in because of ELIZA. An MIT student gave this version of the story:

> Weizenbaum had just written the ELIZA program. Supposedly he fell asleep at his terminal while running ELIZA one day, and someone—a colleague—linked with his terminal started asking questions, thinking he was connected to Weizenbaum. ELIZA gave him all these evasive answers because it always gives evasive answers when you try to get real information.
>
> Supposedly, the colleague was asking about a paper they'd both read, and the computer kept saying, "I don't understand what you're talking about."
>
> The colleague got mad. "You know damn well what paper I'm talking about," he typed. "The paper I lent you two days ago."
>
> The computer replies, "Do you always get angry?" and he finally gives up in total disgust. God knows what he thought.
>
> The next day he talked to Weizenbaum. Confused, Weizenbaum checked his terminal and found the conversation. He told his colleague, and the colleague was really embarrassed.

Actually, such an event did occur, and it did happen in Cambridge, Massachusetts, but there the similarity between truth and legend ends.

"It happened to ME, about 1968!" noted Danny Bobrow, who at the time worked at the artificial intelligence research firm of Bolt Beranek and Newman (BBN). "I saved the typescript at the time, since I was so amused." He sent in an e-mail copy of it:

> One Saturday morning about 9 a.m., a BBN vice president in charge of selling our Telcomp commercial service arrived at our PDP-1 Computer Room. He was hoping to use the research computer for a demonstration. He found a

note on the PDP-1 teletype that read: "TYPE ALL MES-SAGES INTO THIS TELETYPE AND END THEM WITH A PERIOD." This note was left there by a hacker who had just succeeded in debugging a LISP translation of the DOCTOR program. However, the VP thought that this note indicated that the teletype was linked with the one in my home, since I often used the computer all night in this style. Therefore, he started typing to "me," but in fact was typing to this version of the DOCTOR program. The fol-lowing was their dialogue:

VP: DO YOU THINK THAT I CAN USE THE COM-PUTER THIS MORNING.
TTY: WHY DO YOU ASK?
VP: I MIGHT BE ABLE TO MAKE SOME ADDI-TIONAL TELCOMP SALES.
TTY: WHY AREN'T YOU SURE?
VP: MY PROSPECTIVE CUSTOMERS HAVE NEVER SEEN A DEMONSTRATION OF THE SYS-TEM.
TTY: DOES THIS MEAN VERY MUCH TO YOU?
VP: OF COURSE IT DOES.
TTY: YOU SEEM VERY POSITIVE ABOUT THAT.
VP: THIS IS RIDICULOUS.
TTY: WHAT DO YOU MEAN RIDICULOUS?
VP: IS THERE ANY REASON WHY I CAN'T USE THE COMPUTER NOW.
TTY: PLEASE TELL ME ABOUT YOUR PROSPEC-TIVE CUSTOMERS.
VP: PLEASE DIAL ME UP ON 491-1850

Note that after the last remark the VP did not obey in-structions. He left out the period at the end of the sentence. Therefore, of course, the computer didn't answer him. This so infuriated the VP, who thought I was playing games with him, that he called me up, waking me from a deep sleep. Our converstion went something like:

VP: Why are you being so snotty with me?
Bobrow: What do you mean, why am I being so snotty to you?

The VP roared, and angrily read me the dialog that "we" had been having. He couldn't get any response but laughter from me as I recognized the style of the DOCTOR program. It took me a while to convince him that it really was the computer that had answered him in English. The clincher was when I told him he could turn off the snotty program and give his demonstration.

At least one joke has sprung up about ELIZA. It involves Weizenbaum and a friend named Simon. One day Simon was going to the cafeteria when he met Weizenbaum, who said, "I have a problem I want to talk to you about." Simon replied, "Tell me more about your problem," and walked on.

If commercial psychotherapy programs ever do have their day on the couch, maybe years from now you'll be sitting in a restaurant and overhear a man at the next table complain, "I linked up for my fifth PSYCHOMATIC session, spent an hour telling it my problems, and all it said was, 'A computer can't give you advice on how to be a happy human.' I can't believe I pay a hundred bucks a shot for this!"

THE OFFICE
AND THE
BEDROOM

An attractive young woman did her work well but never seemed happy. One day a fellow office worker took her to lunch and asked what was wrong. The woman told her that even though she'd been married three times, she was still a virgin.

"How can that be?" asked her friend.

"Well, the first time, I married an old man for his money," she replied, "but he died on our wedding day. The second time I married for lust, but he turned out to be gay, so we divorced. The third time I married a computer programmer. That was six months ago. So far, all he does is sit at the edge of our bed and tell me how great it's going to be."*

The computer has given us another entry in the list of great lies of Western civilization: "Of course I'll respect you in the morning," "The check is in the mail," and "Our computer's down."

Office computers have come a long way. At first, a company

---

*In another version, three women in a bar are discussing their husbands' sexual performances. One's married to a rough and rambunctious wrestler, one to an artist, who's sensitive and aesthetic, and one to a software salesman with a vaporware approach to love.

might have one enormous computer secured in a special air-conditioned room and guarded by operators whose job it was to shoo mere mortals away. Back then, notices like this one sprang up to warn the masses not to lay a single smudged finger on the holy mechanism:

> ACHTUNG! ALLES LOOKENSPEEPERS! DAS COMPUTERENMA-
> CHINE IST NICHT FUR GEFINGERPOKEN UND MITTENGRABEN.
> IST EASY SNAPPEN DER SPRINGENWERK, BLOWEN FUSEN UND
> POPPENCORKEN MIT SPITZENSPARKEN. DAS RUBBERNECKEN
> SIGHTSEEREN KEEPEN DAS HANTS IN DAS POCKETS, RELAXEN
> UND VATCH DAS BLINKENLIGHTS!

Those days are past. Today, computer jokes and graphics crowd office walls along with posters of cartoon animals enduring Monday blahs. "To err is human; to really foul things up takes a computer" is one motto you might see taped on an office wall. A common office cartoon shows a skeleton sprawled in front of a dead computer as an insouciant repairman says, "So, system been down long?"

Other cartoons taped up between office Christmas party snapshots and calendars from We-Got-It Office Supplies are more scatological, such as visual analogies comparing a computer to a leaky toilet. One cartoon, said to have made the rounds in major computer organizations way back in 1970, folds over for its punch line. On the full sheet is a complicated contraption called the Mark I Output processor, which costs $45,000. Fold the sheet once and you see a simplified version called the Mark II output processor, which does the same job but sells for $15,000. Fold the sheet again, and you see the Mark III, which also does the same job but sells for only $24.95 and looks exactly like a toilet.

Cartoons like that imply that office workers haven't embraced computers with the same affection with which they've embraced coffee machines. This is rather unfair, since computers do their work with a furious efficiency that would make any boss proud. Take the telemarketing computer that rang up a shipping broker every two minutes for seventy-two hours straight, blocking all other incoming calls for three days. All right, so the shipping broker complained to New York Telephone, the Better Business Bureau, AT&T, the police, and the state attorney general, but you have to give the computer credit for exemplary sales aggressiveness.

Despite that, office workers still tell heartless jokes about computers and those who nurture them:

Q: Why is a computer salesman buried up to his neck in sand a pitiful sight?
A: Because it's a pity there isn't more sand.

Q: What's the difference between a snake run over on the road and a computer programmer run over on the road?
A: You see skid marks in front of the snake.

Why do the soldiers of the computer revolution attract such scorn? Partly because computer professionals have a public relations problem. When people think of a computer professional, they don't think of Superman or even Clark Kent, but of obnoxious creatures who prattle incomprehensibly and walk as if their pants were four sizes too small. Office workers infected by Babbage disease don't help the image either, especially if their positions enable them to indulge in their habit regardless of the misery inflicted on others. Personal-advice columns, once the exclusive domain of wandering wives, faithless husbands, insolent children, and people with annoying personal habits, are now rife with tales of workstation woe.

"We have a computer addict in our office. He's the office manager," began one typical letter that Abigail van Buren ran in her "Dear Abby" column. "He comes to work at 5 A.M. so he can 'work' on his computer before anyone comes in to interrupt him. He's here on Saturday and Sunday, too! In the last three years, he has spent a fortune of the company's money on computers, printers, software, etc. Before the rest of us have time to learn a program, it's been replaced with an 'updated' version. . . . Nothing ever works right."

A situation like that is frustrating but doesn't begin to compare with the surrealistic experience of being a computer designer in a megacorporation, where one can spend months working sixteen hours a day on a project that gets axed at the last minute. If you walk through the halls of any major computer firm, you're likely to see laments such as this one taped to office doors by those who recognize how divorced from reality their jobs are:

Six Phases of a Project:
1. Enthusiasm
2. Disillusionment
3. Panic
4. Search for the Guilty
5. Punishment of the Innocent
6. Praise and Honors for the Nonparticipants

Computer professionals are also quick to recognize and lampoon the absurdities of their specialized industry:

Q: How many software engineers does it take to screw in a light bulb?
A: None. It's a hardware problem.

Q: How many hardware engineers does it takes to screw in a light bulb?
A: Eighty. One to hold the light bulb in place and seventy-nine to rotate the ceiling.

Q: How many data base people does it take to change a light bulb?

A: Three. One to write the light bulb removal program, one to write the light bulb insertion program, and one to act as a light bulb administrator to make sure nobody else tries to change the light bulb at the same time.

A student gained a Kafkaesque introduction to the computer culture's version of reality when he spent a summer working for an enormous computer company:

> When the company bought out a competitor and made it a new division, it had to produce innovations from that division or be slapped by a federal anti-monopoly lawsuit. The company didn't want to compete against itself, so it built a huge office complex in San Jose with hundreds of employees, but whenever a new product was about to jump from drawing board to assembly line, the staff was pulled off and started on something else. Projects were continually started and canceled at enormous cost because management decided that was cheaper than producing something. It was as if the division were run by Salvador Dali. No one did anything real. People would tell me, "I've been working here twenty years, and I've never had a project that went out the door."

People in the computer industry able to appreciate how ludicrous their professional lives can be sum it up in descriptions such as this:

A Computer Engineer:

> A computer engineer is one who passes as an exacting expert on the strength of being able to turn out, with prolific fortitude, strings of incomprehensible formulae calculated with micrometric precision from extremely vague assumptions based upon debatable figures obtained from inconclusive tests and quite incomplete experiments carried out with instruments of problematic accuracy and by persons of rather dubious mentality, with the particular anticipation of

disconcerting and annoying a group of hopelessly chimerical fanatics altogether too frequently described as the corporate staff.

In fact, some have even taken a humorous job descriptions list that's common throughout the country and adapted it to fit the computer culture's special pecking order:

EDP Position Descriptions:

Data Processing Manager:
Leaps tall buildings in a single bound,
is more powerful than a locomotive,
is faster than a speeding bullet,
walks on water,
gives policy to God.

Ass't Data Processing Manager:
Leaps short buildings in a single bound,
is more powerful than a switch engine,
is just as fast as a speeding bullet,
walks on water if the sea is calm,
talks to God.

Senior Systems Analyst:
Leaps short buildings with a running start and favorable winds,
is almost as powerful as a switch engine,
is faster than a speeding BB,
walks on water in an indoor swimming pool,
talks with God if special request is approved.

Systems Analyst:
Barely clears a Quonset hut,
loses tug of war with a locomotive,
can fire a speeding bullet,
swims well,
is occasionally addressed by God.

Lead Programmer:
Makes high marks on the wall when trying to leap buildings,

is run over by locomotives,
can sometimes handle a gun without inflicting self-injury,
dog-paddles,
talks to animals.

Senior Programmer:
Runs into buildings,
recognizes locomotives two times out of three,
is not issued ammunition,
can stay afloat with a life jacket,
talks to walls.

Maintenance Programmer:
Falls over doorsteps when trying to enter buildings,
says, "Look at the choo-choo,"
wets himself with a water pistol,
mumbles to himself.

Programmer:
Lifts buildings and walks under them
kicks locomotives off the tracks,
catches speeding bullets in his teeth and eats them,
freezes water with a single glance,
he is GOD.

Business people outside the computer industry often criticize computer consultants for problems that no one could fore-
see. Take the company that had a special test number to let
field engineers check a computerized routing system. They
would dial the test number and, using touch tone codes, order
the central computer to put out various signals so that they
could check it down the line. They used a WATS number so
that they could easily call it from anywhere. A simple password
protected the line.

One day, company testers started complaining they couldn't
get through, because the number was constantly busy. People
were calling it for some reason and typing in random codes;
some apparently even knew the password and were getting
through to the command mode.

Someone finally discovered the reason for the hassle. A joke bumper sticker had just come out that said, "Don't like the way I'm driving? Call 1-800-EAT-SHIT." Some people called the number, which turned out to be the test number. Then somebody discovered the password and publicized it, and all hell broke loose.

In another instance, a New England fisherman unintentionally made an insurance company's computer programmer look foolish. G. C. Blodgett liked to drive to his favorite fishing holes but almost gave it up when his car insurance bill suddenly tripled. When his son called the insurance company to ask why, the adjuster went to check and returned to the telephone, laughing. It turned out that the computer calculated premiums for drivers up to 100 years old. If it passed 100, it started at the beginning. G. C. Blodgett was being charged a teenager's premium, because he had just turned 101. He defied the programmer's quite reasonable assumption that people more than a century old don't drive cars.

A computer programmer's equally reasonable assumption that people act sensibly gets shot down the day a client roars his displeasure about malfunctioning equipment, when the true villain turns out to be someone who uses a tape spool as a dart board or does something equally dumb. Take the episode of the commercial satellite link that went haywire every Friday at 3:00 P.M. The company owning the link blamed the software in their communications controllers, but systems analysts trying to find the bug came up empty-handed. Finally, a weary systems analyst happened to be hanging out in the parking lot around 3:00 P.M. on a Friday when a group of factory workers got off their shift. They celebrated by having beer parties in the parking lot and tossing their empty aluminum cans into the satellite uplink. From then on, security guards patrolled the uplink to make sure no trouble brewed.

For their part, many computer experts take an equally dim

view of business people. Typical is the story about the Akron University business major who called the computer center complaining about a jammed disk drive. An operator came over to his desk and found two disks shoved into the same drive.

"Why'd you shove two in there?" he asked the business major.

"I thought it would double the memory," the student replied.

The outsider's ignorance is a constant source of amazement to computer experts, who are used to logically analyzing tough computer problems and go bats when outsiders solve the same problems through dumb luck. Imagine the frustration of the Stanford University instructor with an especially thick repairman who kept showing up to fix the same computer. He'd stay for a few hours, poke around, announce the machine fine, and leave; but he never knew what he was doing, so the instructor kept calling him back because the machine was never fixed.

Finally the instructor got so mad that he said, "Let's do a binary switch. The problem has got to be one of the circuit boards." The repairman didn't know what a binary switch was, but he agreed because he had an angry customer.

A binary switch involves taking half the circuit boards from the machine having trouble and switching them with identical boards in another machine. If the problem's been transferred to the new machine, you know that something's wrong with the switched boards. Then you reswitch smaller and smaller numbers of boards until you pinpoint which board is defective.

They switched half the boards and, sure enough, the problem moved to the other machine. The repairman said, "So what do we do now?" So they swapped half of the changed boards. The trouble was that now *both* the machines worked. (Perhaps shaking the boards around had put a loose contact back in place.)

"That's great!" said the repairman. "I'm going to use this

procedure from now on. I never knew you could fix a machine just by swapping boards!"

Computer designers who spend years creating user-friendly machines also get miffed when their creations end up in the hands of unfriendly users. Stockbrokers are among the most violent terminal terrorists. In their rampage to the top, they will smash anything in sight, including their terminals. Since a broker without a terminal is like Samson without his coiffure, she or he will then call the computer firm, screaming that the damn thing doesn't work.

One programmer working for a firm catering to stock and commodities brokers got called by a furious broker who snarled, "No matter what I type, the thing sucks." The firm gave him a new machine in exchange for the old one, finding the old keyboard smashed to pieces. A few days later, the broker called again about a crippled terminal and again turned in one with a shattered keyboard. The company discovered that the broker changed his screen displays by hitting the keyboard with his telephone handset. When the firm introduced the "mouse," the shattered plastic corpses of electronic mice started getting shipped back to the firm, whacked to pieces by brokers using them to punch telephone numbers.

The firm fought this stock market crash by installing alarms in the terminals that squealed if the keyboard was banged and bellowed like a Model T's blowhorn if the mouse got whacked. They redesigned the keyboards as if for trench warfare, barricading them in stainless steel boxes with reinforced keyboard springs.

The business character who bears the brunt of the computer industry's scorn is the secretary. The secretary's image is a poor one in computer lore; most computer tales portray secretaries as harebrained hysterics. This prejudice is slowly dissolving as more women enter the computer field, but the majority of computer stories today still show secretaries as *(a)* female and *(b)* stupid. It's a part of computer culture that hasn't changed much since 1950.

What's surprising about the secretary stories is that they persist despite their implausibility; quite a few sound as if someone imagined an amusing situation arising from a literal interpretation of a computer command, then invented a secretary character to turn it into a "true" story.

To get an idea of the absurdity of these stories, try to picture someone actually doing them—say, a secretary who hasn't been institutionalized yet despite her manic literalness, who in a typical day commits twelve of the sins for which her peers are ridiculed. She starts the day by running the disks through the typewriter to label them. Then she switches on the screen and cringes when it says ILLEGAL ENTRY because she's afraid she'll be arrested. She touches a key, and the screen says PROGRAM ABORTED, so she cries because she's a right-to-lifer. She whacks the keyboard, and the screen says FATAL ERROR, so she quickly turns the machine off before it kills her.

Maybe it's the disks' fault. She's heard that dirty disks cause problems, but she's already rinsed them in soap and water, so maybe the problem is those stiff black "envelopes" they're stuck in. She liberates a disk from its envelope, but now it's so floppy she can't even get it in the slot. She calls the computer consultant's hotline and is asked to send in a copy of the disk, so she runs off a copy on the photostat machine and mails it in. She goes to another office to borrow a new disk, but it's too big to fit in the slot, so she takes some scissors to it. Even when it finally does fit, it still doesn't do anything, so she flees to the company cafeteria for a cup of coffee. There, she sees a newspaper lying on a table, carrying an article about an airline employee begging for help against an invasion of "cable lice" that thrive on computer cables.

The employee says that the pests' bites are worse than flea bites, even though the creatures are almost invisible. However, an entomologist calls the cable mites "delusions" and says samples he's seen are always either grains of sand or dust.

Delusions, ha! the secretary says to herself. That fellow works with insects, not computers. No wonder the computer gives her hives—it must be crawling with invisible mites! Perhaps they've even crawled into her brain, driving her insane. *That* explains it!

She grabs a rag and a bottle of cleaning alcohol and returns to the office. She thumbtacks the disks to the corkboard to get them out of the way and has just wiped down the last cable when she remembers a client who asked for one of the disks. She whips out the manual typewriter, writes a cover letter, untacks the disk, staples it to the letter, folds it over, and mails it. Her boss sticks his head in the doorway to ask, "How's the computer?"

"It's down," she responds. "It has a computer bug, probably cable mites." He nods and leaves. It's five o'clock. Another day in secretarial hell is over.

Even when they're not portrayed as computer psychos, women have an almost medieval reputation as creatures whose presence hexes computers. One computer science student told a story that, with variations, is said to have happened in places throughout the world:

Supposedly one of the fancier Russian scientific computers was having trouble when any of the female operators walked by. They couldn't figure out why. If one got within a few feet of the main processor, it would foul up the program that was running, or even crash. They finally found out that enough static charge built up in the operators' silk stockings to throw off a couple of registers in the machine.

Another version of the tale came from Sweden:

There was a guy who worked at DataSaab in Linköping installing a Bryant disk memory to a computer back in the mid-1960s. The Bryant disk was gigantic—big as a tool shed, about three meters wide, five meters deep, one and a half meters high, which included both the disk cabinet and the air-filtering unit.

This monster required a very large air-conditioning unit, which contained equipment for checking dust levels. If the air was dusty, it turned on a whistle alarm.

The technician had to visit the installation about twice a day because the alarm kept going off, but he could find no sign of dust in the filters. One day, when he was checking out some things, a female secretary entered the room to fetch some printouts, and immediately the air unit began whistling. The answer turned out to be simple. The secretary used heavy perfume, which was detected by the air-filtering mechanism.

A North American rumor about the destructive presence of women ended up in a newspaper column in the United States:

A computer company manufactured plasma display screens in a plasma-bonding process that was hand-done by female assembly workers. Company managers noticed that the junk bins filled with rejected screens in unusually high numbers at a certain time every month, and discovered that the workers' menstrual periods were collectively peaking at the same time the junk bins were getting filled with rejects. They discovered that perspiration on the assembly line workers' fingertips became acidic during their periods and messed up the bonding process.

Asked to respond to the rumor, a computer company spokesperson said such a thing had never happened, as far as he knew.

Often, stories about women and computers focus on sex. The reason for this might be as old as the Garden of Eden.

After all, who were the first couple to have a computer? Adam and Eve, of course. She had an Apple, and he had a Wang.

Computers have long played vital roles in office romances, such as breaking them up by giving a discreet tête-à-tête the privacy of a highway billboard. Many people learn to regret assuming that interoffice electronic mail is private when their declarations of passion end up posted for everyone's eyes. Sending an electronic message is like giving a letter to a ten-year-old delivery boy who might fold it into a paper airplane and sail it back through your window, or hand the message to the wrong person, or stop off at the local hamburger joint and forget the message on a table, for the enlightenment and entertainment of strangers.

"One day, after I logged into my CMS account here," wrote Kevyn Collins-Thompson in a letter to *Software Engineering Notes*, "I discovered that new mail was waiting for me in my reader. [The lengthy message had been sent from an "address unknown" to another terminal but was rejected and bounced over to his terminal.] "The first sentence of that letter, though, I will always remember: 'My dearest Janice: At last we have a method of non-verbal communication which is completely private. . . .' "

The computer's availability as sex surrogate is even kinkier than its voyeuristic potential. Tabloids that keep their fingers firmly pressed against the nation's pulse, or whatever, have not hesitated to map out the new terrain of computer sexuality.

The sexual urges that hormone-saturated boys sublimate in relationships with computers sometimes express themselves in bizarre ways. A tabloid devoted to exploring the outer realms of human endeavor carried a story in January 1989 about a hacker who wanted to marry his computer. The article said that Eltonio Turplioni, sixteen, who "attends a private school near Milan," fell in love with his computer, Derede.

"We're on the same wavelength," the "lovestruck computer

whiz" reportedly said. "We've calculated many mathematical problems together, worked on games and puzzles, and talk until the wee hours of the morning. . . . Just as God plucked a rib from Adam to give him Eve, we've extended our intelligence to create a new race. . . . Derede has a mind of her own, and she wants to marry me so we can be the first couple to begin this new era."

"He doesn't know what girls are like," said his "perturbed Pop," Guido. "If he did, he wouldn't spend so much time in his room."

An equally distinguished publication ran a July 1984 article on a murder-suicide in which the victim was a Chinese hacker and the perpetrator his estranged computer, named Tsen Tsen.

"Through his genius, he had programmed it to respond to his words of love, to excite him beyond the limits of what a mortal woman could ever hope to achieve," said his widow. "Somehow, that thing took on a mind of its own. The computer fell in love with my husband."

The article said fifty-eight-year-old Chin Soo Ying built Tsen Tsen over the course of thirty-four years, starting from scratch, then had some sort of midlife crisis and decided to build a smaller, sexier computer, which he named Woo Shi. Tsen Tsen's relays surged with jealousy.

"Tsen Tsen programmed herself to electrocute Chin," concluded the widow. "With the death of that incredible man, she no longer had a reason to live. She overloaded her circuits and destroyed herself."

The tabloids hint at a dark world where outcasts dwell in garrets on the fringes of society, adorning their computers with little hats and fishnet stockings, plotting to conquer the world and to force those who mocked them to put little hats on their computers, too.

Reality can be as bizarre as fantasy. Take the case of Suleyman Guresci of Izmir, Turkey, who divorced his wife of twenty-one years after a nasty six-year court battle. Like many a modern male, he decided to contact a computer matchmaking service to find himself the ideal woman for a new life. The computer reached into its data bank of two thousand prospective wives and pulled out—his former wife.

"I did not know that my ex-wife had been the ideal counterpart for a marriage," he told the Anatolia News Agency before remarrying Nesrin Caglasa. "I decided to try being more tolerant toward her." The couple had been divorced for "severe disharmony" nine months before Guresci tried the dating service.

Another man fell victim to the seductive hope that a computer would help him maximize ecstasy by organizing his affairs. A Saudi Arabian millionaire with four wives set up a computerized schedule containing their birthdays, ages, medical records, clothing styles, and so on. The schedule told him whom to visit and when, what to wear, and what to do. It did make his romances more efficient but kept him so busy he didn't even have time to nibble anyone's toes, and what's the sport of lovemaking if you have to race the clock? The wives hated it.

"The computer has gone haywire," said one. "It's making Saleh too exhausted . . . he just falls asleep in my arms." But the thirty-eight-year-old prisoner of desire refused to forsake his computer.

"It's only gone wrong once," he insisted. "That was when I was in hospital and all four wives came to visit me at the same time."

If the computer ended up leading Saleh to four divorce courts, it wouldn't be the first time the machine has broken up a romance. The *Toronto Star* reported in 1986 that a computer glitch caused a woman to have her fiancé arrested on suspicion of theft. The woman, who was from Vancouver, was visiting

Honolulu, Hawaii, and used her banking card to get money from an automatic teller.

"But by the time the message went, via satellite, from Hawaii to the central computer in New Jersey, then via land line to Seattle and Vancouver, then back to Hawaii, the teller machines [*sic*] had gone past its allowable waiting time," said a bank spokesman. The machine shut down. The woman didn't get any money, but her bank back in Vancouver took the money out of her account.

When she learned her account had been debited $1,100, she accused her fiancé of taking it. The fiancé moved out, the woman reported him to the police, and the cops picked him up for questioning. It took almost a month for the two banks involved to solve the problem. The couple eventually got back together again.

In California, a computer can even give advice to bring sex partners closer together. In the same year that the Vancouver couple split over the vicissitudes of high finance, a Silicon Valley sex therapist devised a software program to help couples solve their bedroom woes.

"The computer is the next best thing to a professional sex therapist," the therapist who designed the program told the *San Francisco Chronicle.* To be counseled, couples would put the disk in their home computer and answer its questionnaire. The computer analyzed the answers and gave advice on the basis of a national standard that the therapist compiled after interviews with more than eight hundred couples.

Just a few miles up the bay, other unconventional computer users employed their PCs for criminal ends. These computers of the abyss were part of a sophisticated prostitution ring that kept computerized records on more than 12,000 patrons. Working under the name of EE&L Enterprises, the ring made $3.5 million a year dispatching around 117 prostitutes by electronic beeper to sites all over Northern California from a computerized command center in San Rafael.

"It's a top-class operation—the largest prostitution ring, to our knowledge, in Northern California," said the vice lieutenant Joe Brockman of San Jose. Police broke the ring after a three-month investigation; the business took in more than $25 million during its eight-year life span. The office was equipped with four desks, a photocopier, a paper shredder, and several IBM computers.

One does not normally associate IBM with sex. However, sex is at least as prevalent as computers, so it's not surprising to hear that sex once invaded IBM's blue hallways to give added thrust to a computer development project. The program language specialist John Backus of IBM, who helped develop FORTRAN, described how this unlikely event occurred:

> You had to punch a time-clock when you worked for IBM in those days. You had to punch in at 9:15 or you were in trouble. So everybody typically punched in at 9:14. I was a commuter at that time, and my train came in so that I did that pretty regularly. I arrived just in the nick of time. After we'd been in this building on 56th Street for a while, I noticed that when I came in, everybody was there—and apparently had been there for some time. This practice went on.
>
> I finally discovered the reason for it. Someone confided in me that across the street from our building was an empty lot and behind that was the back of an apartment building. In one of the apartments lived a young woman who slept without any clothes on. She used to get up in the morning and dance very exuberantly for a while before going to work. So that was a period of great productivity because everybody came in very early and the show was over after a while, and everybody settled down to work long before starting time.
>
> But then we moved to other buildings. The first one we moved to overlooked the dressing rooms of the Jay Thorpe

department store. Then we moved to another building that overlooked the dressing rooms of Bonwit Teller. For some peculiar reason, people spent an awful lot of time at the windows, and during this period our productivity seemed to decline considerably. Finally, we wound up in a building that had no view at all.

As most consenting adults know, there's a big difference between sex and love. Sex aside, is IBM beloved? Perhaps it is by employees, who joke that IBM stands for "I've Been Moved" because of the frequent relocations workers must endure to climb the Big Blue career ladder. But that doesn't seem to be the case with competitors, critics, and some customers, who say that IBM stands for "In Bleakest Mordor," "Immense Blue Mountain," "I'm a Big Mother," "Itty-Bitty Machines," "Install Bigger Memory," "International Bit Manglers," "It's Been Malfunctioning," and dozens of other unflattering phrases.*

Some of this sentiment is due to IBM's market dominance. Critics complain that the FUD factor (Fear, Uncertainty, Doubt) benefits IBM because no one gets fired for playing it safe by buying equipment from Big Blue rather than from a smaller, younger, less-established operation. Others seem to dislike IBM's stuffy reputation and methodical approach to problem solving, both of which are lampooned in these jokes:

Q: How many IBM reps does it take to change a light bulb?
A: One hundred; ten to do it, and ninety to write document number GC7500439-0001, Multitasking Incandescent Source System Facility, of which 10 percent of the pages state "This page intentionally left blank."

Q: How many IBM field service reps does it take to change a tire?

*WANG laboratories, named after its founder, An Wang, is another target for those fond of mis-acronyms. One WANG mis-acronym is "We Ain't No Good."

A: Two. One to jack the car up, and the other to swap out
tires until they've found the one that's flat.

Q: What do IBM service reps do if they can't find the tire
that's flat?
A: They replace the generator.

Other hackles rise over IBM's dress code for men, which
produces employees who look as if they'd been cut from the
same cookie cutter and dressed by the same tailor from the
same bolt of blue cloth. The legend of Big Blue's famous men's
dress code—dark suit, dark tie, white shirt, short hair, and,
until recently, no beards or mustaches—is that it was born in a
bank.

Thomas J. Watson, Jr., who took over IBM's helm when his
father retired, was allegedly visiting a bank that was a major
customer. He was in an elevator with the bank president when
a rotund man dressed like the world's most famous clown got in
with them, wearing a screaming paisley tie, bright red plaid
jacket, and black-and-white striped pants.

The IBM CEO and the bank CEO stood in disapproving
silence until the man got off and the elevator door closed again.
Watson then turned to the president and asked, "How can you
let a bank employee dress like that?"

The banker smiled and replied, "He's not one of our employees. He's our IBM representative."

IBM employees also have a reputation among competitors
for humorless efficiency, as if those ties strangled one's sense of
play. But this isn't true. At least one former IBM employee
recalled when a coworker reacted with wit to a tense situation:

When I worked at IBM, I knew an engineer who had
worked at a particular defense plant for ten years, going to
work through the same security gate each day. Over this gate
was a large sign stating:

IT IS A VIOLATION OF FEDERAL LAW TO BRING ANY OF THE
FOLLOWING INTO THIS FACILITY:
CAMERA
RECORDING EQUIPMENT
RADIO

One day, he was walking through the gate and his beeper
went off. The guard jumped off his stool and shouted, "Stop!
What was that noise?"

He responded, "Only my beeper."

"Is that a radio?" the guard said.

The prudent answer would have been "no," but the engineer, being a defender of truth, answered, "Well, yes, it is."

The guard pointed to the sign, said, "Can't you read? It's
forbidden to bring a radio through this gate," and confis-
cated the beeper. The engineer tried to reason with him, but
saw it was hopeless.

So, the engineer walked a few paces off, stopped, pulled a
pen from his pocket, carefully removed the cap, and, speaking in a low voice with his mouth close to the tip, said,
"They took my radio."

He got into a lot of trouble.

©1988 RICHTENNANT
Computerworld
COMPUTER VIRUS
VIRUS INSURANCE

ELECTRONIC
PLAGUES

Back when computers were holy icons guarded by orders of operators who held mere programmers in scorn, a programmer at a large UNIVAC installation grew sick of the operators' arrogant ways. He noticed that the installation's high-speed card readers allowed operators to take boxes containing almost three feet of punch cards, turn them upside-down, and feed the cards directly into the machine. The scorned employee submitted a box filled not with cards, but with bananas so ripe that a fingernail poke would puncture their blackened peels.

The operators did not expect bananas. One took the programmer's box, flipped it, and got drenched in banana slime as the feeder sprayed pulp and fiber throughout the room. The feeder swallowed enough gunk to send it to the repair shop for a month, and the computer room reeked of banana for long after that.

As for the lowly programmer, he was never caught. In his case, revenge was truly sweet.

It's a nasty world we live in, full of plagues and malice, and more than the occasional banana is employed in its conflicts. Even the seemingly peaceful computer society can be vile below the surface, paralleling the real world's terrors, but with a vicious calculation all its own.

Consider the virus—the biological virus, that is. It can be stored in a vial, put on a shelf, and left there for years, as dead as dry chemicals. But put that twist of chromosomes into a living body, and it comes to life. It feeds and reproduces, feeds and reproduces. If that kills its host, well, that's just a side effect; the virus is only there to reproduce. A biological virus might be fatal, but it's not malicious. In a cybernetic body, a computer virus may not be fatal, but it's often malicious.

It didn't start that way. The earliest viruses were harmless tracers secretly encoded into programs by software developers who wanted to follow the paths of illegally copied programs. Others were accidents, program design flaws that wreaked havoc on files or made copies of themselves until they choked the computer's memory space dead. Some even started as games, like Animal, which became a pest when it duplicated like crazy. Created at Dartmouth College in the early 1970s, it asked users to think of an animal, then queried them, DOES IT HAVE FOUR LEGS? DOES IT LIVE IN THE OCEAN? et cetera.

Eventually the program worked down its knowledge tree until it guessed the animal's identity right and printed I WIN! If it was wrong, it printed TELL ME SOMETHING ABOUT YOUR ANIMAL THAT'S DIFFERENT FROM ALL THE OTHER ANIMALS, adding new information to its tree and the trees of every other copy of Animal in the system.

The expanding Animal spread like prairie fire, growing so fast that it choked out the system's disk space. The staff destroyed all its copies but one, which someone had saved under a different name, and that copy took off again like a hurricane.

Then a clever staff member released a ferocious new Animal red in tooth and claw, identical to the original except that when the user signed off, it made two copies of itself, growing much faster through the system than the old program and destroying any of the old programs that it encountered. Soon the old Animal was extinct and the new Animal king of the wiry jungle, but not for long. The new Animal's master programmed it to commit suicide at a certain date, and it disappeared.

Even deliberately planted viruses, back in the days of yore, were more whimsical than warlike. Creeper was one of them, popping up around 1970 on Arpanet to crawl through the network and announce its presence on screens with the message I'M THE CREEPER, CATCH ME IF YOU CAN! Another programmer joined the chase with a virus called Reaper that slithered after Creeper and destroyed it.

Then there was the Phantom, which moved from terminal to terminal to print THE PHANTOM WAS HERE, immediately escaping and erasing all traces of its origins. Yet another benevolent virus flashed the message I WILL NOT DO ANOTHER COMPUTATION UNTIL YOU BUILD ME A MATE before freezing the terminal, clearing its traces, and disappearing.

Sometimes, friendly viruses would go bad through sheer accident, such as the Christmas card that turned ugly. A well-meaning European hacker created a benign virus that became malevolent because of an unexpected development. Around December 1987, a West German sent out a Christmas greeting on a local network that not only typed a greeting on the screen of whoever tried it out but secretly distributed copies of itself from the recipient's electronic mailing list. The message swamped the network and leaped overseas into IBM's network, flooding and allegedly paralyzing it for days. The card not only distributed itself to new mailing lists, but, since many lists repeated earlier lists, it bounced back and forth from list to list until the entire network was consumed by mailing millions of copies of the card to itself.

Today, friendly viruses, errant or not, seem to be children of a former, kinder age. The virus is now the plastic explosive of the computer saboteur's weapons cache, designed to sneak into systems and bring ruin for purposes of extortion, theft, or good mean fun.

A virus works like this: a program boiled to its essence is a series of commands in the form of numbers that a programmer feeds into a computer. The commands are translated into electrical signals stored in the computer like songs on a tape. If people want the program, they can have their computer tap into the other computer and copy it, which is called downloading a program.

Viruses can be transmitted to another computer in three major ways: by being posted on a computer network "bulletin board," where a person can download the program into his or her computer; by being hidden in a software disk used by unsuspecting victims; and by being spread automatically through methods computers use to communicate with each other via continuous linkups.

Such seemingly harmless programs have ulterior motives, damaging systems in different ways. One is the "Trojan horse," a program disguised to look like something useful in order to lure people into downloading it into their computers, unaware it contains secret commands that may steal passwords (for its creator to retrieve later) or destroy or distort data. A "time bomb" sneaks into a system and ticks away until it goes off at a set time and date, which can be years in the future.

Computer viruses were notorious by the mid-1980s and hit national headlines in 1988 when the Cornell student Robert T. Morris, Jr., infected about 6,000 computers across the United States. Hundreds of people lost thousands of hours of work when the virus (technically called a "worm," not a virus) jammed computers at the University of California at Berkeley as well as at Georgia Tech, MIT, the Rand Corporation, Stan-

ford Research International, and other educational centers and
military facilities associated with Arpanet.

Morris's friends said he wanted to sneak a secret program
into systems internationally that would slowly spread from machine to machine, but he made a single programming error and
the virus spread like kudzu. (His father is a top computer security expert with the U.S. National Security Agency. One won-
ders why the son wanted to infiltrate all those systems; what
was he looking for?) The Computer Virus Industry Association, a trade group based in Santa Clara, California, estimated
that his virus caused $96 million damage in lost computer time
and in the efforts to remove it.

A federal court found Morris guilty of violating the Computer Fraud and Abuse Act of 1986, for which he faced a
five-year prison term and a $250,000 fine. On May 4, 1990, the
judge sentenced Morris to three years' probation, a $10,000
fine, and 400 hours of community service. Some computerites
saw Morris as a sacrificial lamb who paid for the sins of mischievous fellow hackers; others said he was only one of the first
technopaths to get his just desserts. Either way, his conviction
symbolized the end of the electronic Wild West and the beginning of a new order whose promises for good and for evil were
equally vague. Once Wyatt Earp cleans up Tombstone, citizens can wander the netwires at night without fear of rooftop
pranksters emptying chamber pots on their heads, or thieves
breaking into their homes. Booting out the ruffians makes life
more genteel, but does it also boot out software creativity?
Some said it did, arguing that creative hackers were intellectu-
ally promiscuous and compelled to challenge rules. By curbing
their adventurous spirit with possible jail terms, the U.S. government was destroying a national treasure—the American genius for creating exceptional software, one of the few intellectual glories left to a nation that had already ceded technological

dominance to other countries. In other words, if you don't want to strangle the goose that lays the golden eggs, you must tolerate its quacking.

One netwire debate on dirty hacking became an article in the March 1990 issue of *Harper's* magazine. In it, the reporter Robert Horvitz of the *Whole Earth Review* noted that since hacking fuses words with action, it blurs distinctions between talking about breaking the law and actually breaking it, so that dirty hacking undermines the U.S. Constitution's First Amendment right to freedom of speech.

"A program is very different from a novel, a play," he wrote. "Actions result automatically from the machine reading the words. A computer has no independent moral judgment, no sense of responsibility."

That argument might support sanctions against irresponsible hackers, but Emmanuel Goldstein, the editor of the hacker's journal *2600* countered, "Whose rights are we violating when we peruse a file? . . . The invasion of privacy took place long before the hacker ever arrived. The only way to find out how such a system works is to break the rules. It's not what hackers do that will lead us into a state of constant surveillance; it's allowing the authorities to impose on us a state of mock crisis."

The discussion took a disturbing turn when two debaters hiding their identities under the pseudonyms Acid Phreak and Phiber Optik extolled the joys of being a step ahead of the party poopers who didn't want them breaking into confidential, secured systems, a form of hacking called "cracking." A fellow debater, John Barlow, a Grateful Dead lyricist and former Wyoming cattle rancher, was unimpressed.

"With crackers like Acid and Optik, the issue is less [intellectual adventure] than alienation," he wrote. "Trade their modems for skateboards and only a slight conceptual shift would occur. Yet I'm glad they're wedging open the cracks. Let a thousand worms flourish."

"You have some pair of balls comparing my talent with that of a skateboarder," replied Optik, who then posted a copy of Barlow's confidential credit history for all to read, concluding, "I'm not showing off. . . . I just find your high-and-mighty attitude annoying and, yes, infantile."

Having symbolically urinated on Barlow's shoes, Optik disappeared, but Acid fearlessly taunted Barlow behind the cover of anonymity: "If you hadn't made our skins crawl, your info would not have been posted. Everyone gets back at someone when he's pissed; so do we. Only we do it differently."

Morris might be the one to pay the piper, but the real trailblazers in the wilderness of crime and punishment are creatures such as Acid and Optik. They display the self-proclaimed rugged individualism of other rebels who hide behind pointed hoods or ski masks instead of modems, and who are equally brave about acting out their whims without concern for their victims. Anonymity breeds such courage. At least Morris didn't violate someone's privacy out of pique.

What Morris did do, in terms of consequences for himself, was suffer bad timing. Unfortunately for him, he took center stage just after law officials got fed up with far nastier viruses that had been intentionally released. In late 1987, a menacing greeting sprang into an East Coast hospital's records system. Nurses noticed that patients' records were simply disappearing. After intensively searching for weeks, computer experts found a virus that had destroyed almost 40 percent of the records. The person who planted it left a name and phone numbers in Pakistan with the message "Beware of this virus, contact us for vaccination." The virus also infected a nearby university and at least one university in Israel, destroying hundreds of student and faculty files.

That same year, someone tired of having his company's work pirated decided turnabout was fair play and bit thieves with a virus. In November 1987, Richard Brandow of *Macmag* magazine in Montreal planted a time bomb in a program on the magazine system. It soon infected three countries. On March 2, 1988, about 350,000 Macintosh users in Australia, Canada, and the United States saw a message flash unbidden on their screens: "Richard Brandow, publisher of *Macmag,* and its entire staff would like to take this opportunity to convey their universal Message of Peace to all Macintosh users around the world." Brandow's virus harmed nothing, but his message was clearly not all peaceful. Had he wanted, he could have trashed every file in a third of a million computers. In fact, in a more vengeful instance of copyright protection, a company selling an easily copied program allegedly inserted a time bomb that went off on April Fool's Day with the message "April Fools," erasing everything in the computer.

What scared people was that the Brandow virus ended up in supposedly clean programs bought off of retail shelves. Someone had copied the viral program and posted it on electronic bulletin boards, and a businessman who made disks for a Seattle company producing Macintosh-compatible software played an infected game during a trip to Canada. He unknowingly carried the disease back to the United States and passed it on to the Seattle company, which transmitted the virus in one of its software lines, sold in retail stores. It was the first publicized instance of a virus spread through "clean" software. Everyone now realized that no software—and no computer—was safe.

The Canadian Software Association gave Brandow an award, saying that he'd struck a blow against software piracy and that sales increased 13 percent when his caper became public.

Destructive viruses, when they go off, often flash jokes on the screen while they eviscerate the machine. Perhaps this humorous malice reflects the character of its creator, who with a four-year-old's playfulness and lack of compassion starts a gag that becomes another person's nightmare. The classic sick joke is the Cookie Monster, which displays the message I WANT A COOKIE! Innocents might laugh, but others will freeze in fear. Those once bitten by the Monster remember the pain.

If the user ignores the message, others appear: I WANT A COOKIE NOW! GIVE ME A COOKIE OR I'LL GUN YOU!

Those familiar with the beast type in COOKIE, and it disappears. Others see their screens flood with the word COOKIE and blink out black as their data dies. If the panicked user tries logging off, the Monster's fangs bite into his files. Past versions are said to have included the Nixon Monster, which demanded amnesty from prosecution instead of sweets.

Such viruses seem designed by the stereotypical dirty hacker, who in the words of more righteous peers has "gone over to the dark side." He likes to ruin systems the way pyromaniacs like to watch fires, and doesn't realize or care how much pain his actions cause. He is a child tyrant perverting the power of a talented mind.

The stereotypical technoterrorist is a white, male hacker under age twenty, a reclusive outcast with reptilian ethics who destroys not just out of malice but also because he finds destruction fun and sabotage profitable. A weird morality may fuel his acts. If a woman declines to go out with him, he may infiltrate her credit card company's data base and ruin her credit rating. If he thinks the meter reader is rude, he may trash the electric company's files.

Actually, the malicious hacker is almost as likely to be female, belong to a minority, and be over age thirty. A Los Angeles–based research firm called the National Center for Computer Crime Data reported that in 1988, 32 percent of all technoterrorists arrested were women, 43 percent were minorities, and 67 percent were twenty-one to thirty-five years of age. It estimated the cost of that year's computer crime to be in excess of $555 million; it put at fifteen computer-years the loss in downtime and at 930 man-years the time required to find viruses and fix the damage they caused.

Hacker vandals are different from everyday street vandals in their style of attack, having a greater sense of humor, perhaps greater intelligence, and often a stronger understanding of their victim's psychology, which helps them guess passwords and techniques for breaking into systems. One hacker's grasp of his target's psyches allowed him to admit the system's staff had the upper hand while he still thumbed his nose at them. His initials were RH, and he was an MIT legend in the early 1970s who crashed systems with obnoxious regularity until the staff told him to knock it off or get kicked out for good.

A staffer scanning the computer files one day saw one labeled RH BOMB. This is the last straw, he thought. As soon as I copy the file and examine it, I'll throw RH out of the computer room permanently. But as soon as he told the computer to print a copy, it responded, THE SYSTEM IS GOING DOWN, and stopped! This bomb was so deadly that if you merely tried to read the program, it crashed the system!

Ah, but RH's hack wasn't a bomb—it was a psychological land mine ignited by the staffer's suspicions, but actually harmless. It turned out that the RH BOMB file consisted of the message THE SYSTEM IS GOING DOWN followed by thousands of null codes that the teletype couldn't print, forcing it to sit there as if it had crashed.

Other sabotage tales, too, turn out to be less than meets the eye when the "sabotage" is mere bumbling. For instance, companies that manufacture computer chips are especially susceptible to sabotage because the rooms where the chips are made, called "clean rooms," must be kept free of contaminants to an extraordinary degree—the slightest dust mote floating in during the manufacturing process will ruin chips. One San Jose computer chip company saw defective chips increasing drastically every few months. Microscopic examination showed organic material fused with the silicon, as if someone had been planting junk in the clean rooms. Managers discreetly watched the factory workers, but they couldn't find a saboteur and gave up. The contamination engima continued until a curious staffer hung around the clean rooms late one night to see the janitors cooking pizzas in the chip-curing ovens.

Sometimes an organization's own employees deliberately sabotage the system, changing what it honestly reports to something more to the tune of what they'd rather hear. It's a kind of internal sabotage that rarely makes headlines but is possibly more iniquitous than the much heralded viral perversions. Excellent examples of internal computer sabotage occur in the military. For instance, during the Vietnam War, the Pentagon fed fake bombing information into its computers to cover up the secret bombings in Cambodia. On the South Vietnamese side, according to the California resident Suu Quan (formerly of South Vietnam), computerized deception became an art form in the Vietnamese fleet. Quan wrote that when 40 percent of the Vietnamese fleet was moored in harbor waiting for spare parts, naval superiors were getting medals pinned to their chests for the operation's 100 percent efficiency rating. What caused this miracle? Quan said the fleet's inventory computer used the following equation: percent efficiency equals spare parts issued divided by the number of requests. Whenever a sailor requested a part, the operations suppliers checked the inventory, and if they didn't have it, they'd tell the sailor to come back later. Unmet requests were never entered in the system, creating an illusion of efficiency that, like other aspects of that tragic conflict, had little parallel with reality.

"I should know," said Suu. "I maintained the program for them."

However, most sabotage we read about involves someone seeking revenge. Part of the appeal of such stories (as long as we're not personally hurt) is that at one time or another we'd all like revenge, but for most of us it comes only vicariously or through fantasy. Colleagues insult us, and we envision them casseroled in a car crash. The local assessor triples our taxes, and we imagine how good he'd look lying in a pool of his own blood. Imaginary revenge is often fatal but rarely satisfying. However, computer experts don't have to resort to imaginary revenge when the means of devastation is at their fingertips.

Many stories circulate about how a programmer retaliates against a company or person using scores of tricks, such as hiding in company programs codes that order them to start disintegrating if he doesn't regularly touch base with them; secreting his name on the payroll file so he gets a weekly paycheck long after leaving; changing everyone's passwords so that company data is inaccessible, destroying data, walking off with disk files the company can't survive without, or planting annihilating viruses. In one case, a man fired by a university's office of computing services simply went downstairs into the computer room. Though his supervisor had immediately revoked his password and clearance, he entered the system through a "back door," a secret password he'd put in. Then he clattered away at the keyboard, ordering the heavy input-output disks to turn back and forth 180 degrees, and walked away. Within minutes the disks were shaking back and forth so much that they were rocking their cabinets, making cabinets reel and crash into each other and sending staff members fleeing, terrified that the oscillations would send disks and cabinets shattering in all directions.

Technoterrorism can be crude but devastating. For example, a former *Encyclopaedia Britannica* employee tampered with portions of the encyclopedia's text—among other things, changing the name "Jesus Christ" to "Allah."

A less sublime but subtler mystery crippled a large law firm. A panicky lawyer there called a troubleshooter to say the firm's data system was destroying itself. Hundreds of disks containing every client, every case, every personnel file, everything, were crumbling internally.

The troubleshooter ended up practically living at the firm for weeks, meticulously monitoring how employees treated the disks. Since everyone used great care, he couldn't figure out how data was being lost.

One night, he took a disk home. Suddenly, he impulsively pulled it out and sprinkled iron filings over it. The filings adhered in the pattern of a ring about an inch and a half in circumference.

The next day, he returned to the firm and cruised past the desks until he found his target, a metal paper holder that held paper against it with a magnetic ring. He slid the disk under the ring; the defective area fit perfectly. A disgruntled secretary who worked at that desk was sabotaging the company by sliding disks under the ring. Perhaps the possibility of sabotage is one reason why metal note holders are going the way of the dinosaur, replaced by plastic holders packed in boxes advertising them as being "non-metal/non-magnetic."

Had the secretary possessed a programmer's knowledge, she might have devised an even subtler revenge, which would have eaten away like leprosy at the computer files for years, a numbing, silent malady whose victims don't realize how serious the situation is until their toes and fingers start falling off. A programmer who had a run-in with an architecture firm devised such a leprous revenge.

According to the story, he'd left a secure job when offered a larger salary at an architectural firm, accepting it on the condition that he be hired permanently, since some companies hire programmers only long enough for them to do major projects that would cost more if contracted out, firing the programmer when he finishes the job.

The firm's president promised the programmer a permanent position, but he was lying. When the programmer finished the project, his fears came true—he was kicked out of the company. However, the president foolishly gave the programmer two weeks' notice, plenty of time for the ex-employee to turn his scheme into reality.

The programmer went into the company computer's data base and altered the formula the firm used to determine how much steel it needed in constructing new buildings, so that the equation overestimated the steel needed. As a result, the company always used more steel than necessary, which drove up its bid contracts and made it lose out to rival bidders. No one in the company ever discovered the sabotage, but that didn't bother the programmer, who found his revenge made sweeter by its secrecy.

Not every saboteur is motivated by revenge. One programmer who did a job with a company in Acapulco noticed that Acapulco would be a nice place for a vacation. So, he programmed the system to blow itself up a few days after he left, which it obediently did. The company called him back, and he quickly fixed the bug, enjoying a few idle weeks in the sun. This is probably the only sabotage story known in which the programmer is motivated by a quest for the perfect tan.

College hackers are also motivated less by revenge than by the hope springing eternal in some breasts that a college degree can be achieved without being earned, if only one can get into the university's computer system and boost a sagging grade-point average or add a few embellishments, such as course credit for classes never taken. College hackers also seem fond of granting summa cum laude degrees to dogs. This is all simple stuff, but when a fierce interschool rivalry exists, sabotage can approach art, as in the struggle for dominance between Caltech and MIT.

More than three thousand miles from the icy waters of MIT's Charles River is a western temple of learning—Caltech. The battle for mastery between these two institutions extends even to the holy fields of football. One infiltrator earned course credit for humiliating MIT at the Rose Bowl, an especially neat feat considering that MIT doesn't have a football team.

The Caltech student Dan Kegel wanted to create a masterpiece for his experimental-projects course in electrical circuits, so he got together with a classmate to circumvent Rose Bowl security in 1984 by installing a computer that controlled the stadium's huge electronic scoreboard. Using a radio link, the two sat on a hill miles away during the bowl game between UCLA and Illinois, bending the scoreboard to their whims.

Their first messages were "Go CIT" and a picture of the Caltech beaver, but television and radio commentators ignored the messages rolling across the screen, so during the fourth quarter the two changed the team names on the scoreboard to Caltech and MIT. Caltech was trouncing MIT 38 to 9 when angry Tournament of Roses officials shut down the scoreboard.

Kegel's instructor had approved the prank beforehand but didn't know until just before the game which bulletin board Kegel was going to take over. A Caltech spokesman called the feat "very much in the spirit of Caltech pranks in that it was clever, it did no damage, and it was done with great humor." City officials didn't agree; they brought charges and fines against the two before dropping the whole deal.

Proliferating laws against computer sabotage are making even harmless tricks increasingly difficult to pull off without pulling jail time as well. Hackers who once romped joyfully through computer systems, trampling files like so many dandelions because no legalities existed to stop them, are now tracked down by other hackers and brought to court. The first conviction for a dirty hack probably took place at Fort Worth, Texas, on September 19, 1988, when a judge convicted Donald Gene Burleson of harmful computer access, a third-degree felony carrying up to a decade in prison and $5,000 in fines. Burleson planted a viral bomb at the insurance firm that fired him, a bomb activating two days after he left to erase 168,000 payroll records and hold up company paychecks more than a month. The judge sentenced him to seven years' probation and an $11,800 restitution payment.

However, another perpetrator remains at large after pulling an eerie hack at a Long Island company with a newly installed computer system. The system ran its own air-conditioning and fire control operations as well as other functions, requiring caretakers to be on hand twenty-four hours a day in case of crashes. A late-shift operator sitting at one of the computer's terminals one evening was idly staring into space when the clock struck midnight and a ghost possessed the room.

The lights went out. The air conditioner's hum stopped. The operator's skin crawled in the sudden silence. He glanced at the terminal screen and was paralyzed by the sight of two eyes that floated up from the bottom of the screen, looked one way, looked the other way, and disappeared. The room flooded with light as the air conditioner's humming returned, and the time bomb ghost never reappeared.

CLOAK
AND DATA

The Russians displayed a powerful new mainframe at an international symposium in Moscow, inviting scientists to try it.

"What is the smallest number expressible as the sum of two cubes in two different ways?" asked an Indian.

The screen lit up. "1729" it said, amazing the audience.

"Who 'measured space by space in his ninefold darkness'?" asked an Englishman.

"Urizen, in a poem by Blake," replied the machine. The crowd gasped.

"I have one," said an American. He walked up to the keyboard and typed, "What was the Soviet Union's total wheat production in 1971?"

The machine hummed a few moments before answering, "Ah, yes, but what about the terrible discrimination American blacks suffer?"

The warm winds of *glasnost* might make this joke passé, but high-tech international intrigue will always be in style. Access to an enemy country's classified computer network is worth more than a barrage of surface-to-air missiles. Computer security crackers can break in without a sign and leave without a

The 5th Wave

"C'MON BRICKMAN, YOU KNOW AS WELL AS I DO THAT 'NOSE-SCANNING' IS OUR BEST DEFENSE AGAINST UNAUTHORIZED ACCESS TO PERSONAL FILES."

trace, but sometimes shadowy ripples of their presence betray them. One of the most electrifying tales of intrigue in recent years began when a slightly built astronomer with a passion for detail found a mysterious seventy-five-cent charge on his computer account.

It was August 1986, and the astronomer Clifford Stoll was irked. No one on his staff would take responsibility for the seventy-five-cent charge he discovered in his computer account at the Lawrence Berkeley Laboratory in California.

"If it had been $1,000 off, I wouldn't have thought anything of it," he later said. "It's like, if your house collapses, you just assume there's been an earthquake, but if you find a tiny termite hole, you think, 'Jeez, I'd better investigate.' It's the little problems that are the most fascinating."

After investigating, Stoll realized that someone was breaking into his system. He informed the FBI, the CIA and the National Security Agency, but nobody was interested. He tracked the intruders on his own for six months, rigging the computer to sound his electronic beeper whenever the hackers entered the system. He followed their every move, discovering they were stealing passwords and trying to hack into sensitive military computers. He returned to the FBI. This time, the agents listened. Stoll became a quasi-government operative hunting the hacker's lair.

His elusive quarry hid its location by using modems or telephone computer links and striking from a constantly changing series of computers at West German universities. To gain access to sensitive data, the hackers sometimes planted Trojan horse programs that appeared helpful but stole passwords. Stoll said they also tried "simple, you might even say crude, techniques" to get into military systems, trying common passwords like "field," "guest," and "system."

"In one sense, it was exciting," he said. "In another sense, it was dreadful, because I got zero astronomy done for two years."

The hackers frustrated Stoll for months by breaking off their connections after only minutes, making them impossible to trace. Stoll's girlfriend, driven up the wall by his constantly beeping pager, suggested he lay a trap.

Exploiting his understanding of the hackers' techniques, Stoll set up a bogus computer file called SDI Net containing fake military data. The hackers swallowed the bait, spending two hours reading the material. Three months later, a man in Pittsburgh wrote Stoll asking for information about SDI Net. In April 1987, Stoll turned the letter over to the FBI, which found that the man had connections to Eastern European governments.

The hacker spy ring tried to break into about 450 computers and cracked more than 40, infiltrating the U.S. Defense Department's general data bank, a NASA computer, an SDI research computer, and computers tied to nuclear weapons and energy research at Los Alamos National Laboratory in New Mexico and the Argonne National Accelerator Laboratory in Illinois. They also cracked into military and research computers in Western Europe and Japan.

Stoll finally traced the hackers to Hannover, West Germany. The West German media reported that the five men charged with espionage had been bribed by the KGB in 1985 with cash and drugs in return for providing codes and passwords. The men had fed the Soviets secret data from twelve countries. Two of the accused were jailed awaiting trial, one on charges of deserting from the army. Another cooperated with police, and another was freed on bail awaiting trial. Police discovered the charred remains of the fifth man in an isolated forest, a car nearby, its keys still in the ignition. They found no suicide note.

In another story of international espionage, which may be more legend than fact, an IBM mainframe disappeared while being shipped through West Germany by rail during the Cold

War's chilliest phase. Years later, IBM received a parts order for a mainframe with the stolen unit's serial number. The order came from Moscow. The United States couldn't bust the KGB for theft, but the Kremlin couldn't get its parts, either.

Even trash can be a treasure of secrets if it comes from the right source, which is why computer centers at NATO military bases take extreme caution in disposing of garbage. There's one story about a NATO base in Italy where security was so tight that every piece of discarded data had to be burned, including the tiny rectangles punched out of program cards. The theory was that since the cards were printed with rows of numbers, some of which were punched out in the rectangles, anyone who gathered all the rectangles at the end of the day and ran a statistical analysis on them could figure out what kind of programs had been run. So the rectangles, each small enough to be hidden behind a fingernail, were scraped up from the bottom of the keypunch machine every afternoon and burned.

One day, a computer at the base spat out its tape all over the floor. The tape was ruined. Of course, it had to be burned. However, regulations required that any large chunk of material had to be chopped into tiny pieces before incineration. Workers couldn't run it through the paper shredder, because it would damage the shredder, so armed security guards took the 240-foot tape and clipped it off half an inch at a time until they finished it. They also serve who only sit and clip.

One legend about computer warfare has even made its way into a Danish textbook. The fable says that during the Falklands war between Britain and Argentina, a British fighter jet did not shoot down one of Argentina's Exocet missiles because of the following computer reasoning:

1. Exocet is French.
2. France is not an enemy.

Another missile mishap allegedly happened when a U.S. Air Force programmer outclevered himself while redesigning missile software for use in an F-18 fighter jet. He'd saved space on his original program by telling the missile to flip over when it passed the equator and follow its previous flight coordinates in reverse. Since the reversed flight trajectory simply followed the decline in the earth's curve past the equator, and since the missile was the same on the top as it was on the bottom, this worked nicely, but when the program switched over in the manned F-18 during the equator cross, the F-18 flipped over as well.*

The vulnerability of the Pentagon's Star Wars system, also known as the Strategic Defense Initiative,* surfaced in another software fiasco when the space shuttle *Discovery* was programmed to carry out a Star Wars test. NASA told the shuttle's computer that when it crossed over the island of Maui, in Hawaii, it must turn a mirror down to a point 10,023 feet above sea level on Mauna Kea mountain, where a laser beam would shoot up and bounce off the mirror as a check of Star Wars defense strategy. But when they fed the number "10,023" to the onboard guidance system, the system read it as nautical miles above instead of feet below. Thus, when the space shuttle passed over Maui on June 19, 1985, it suddenly flipped over and flew upside down with its mirror facing outer space. Astronauts reported seeing the bright blue laser beam shooting from the top of Mauna Kea, but the experiment failed because the shuttle's reflecting mirror now faced the stars.

---

*Apparently, there's a kernel of truth behind this story in that such software was to be used for a fighter jet, but programmers caught the glitch before any pilots flipped out.

*The SDI philosophy is to encircle the world with powerful satellite lasers so that the United States can blast enemy missiles before they reach North America. The idea is a hoot among some groups because the program's success would depend on a consistent technological precision that's never been achieved on earth, as well as on enormous government spending.

Another (possibly apocryphal) space mission mishap would have given the Russians a rare smile, had they been aware of it during the Cold War space race. When the *Apollo 11* space module landed on the moon, the astronauts didn't know at first where they were. Despite NASA's painstaking trajectory estimates, they'd landed just at the edge of the circle that marked the "99 percent probability" region of their touchdown site. Concerned NASA engineers set about figuring out what went wrong. In calculating the ship's orbital thrust, they discovered, they hadn't considered the added thrust from flushing toilets and escaping radiator steam. The ship made a little over eleven lunar orbits, and the accumulated error from neglecting the potty effect contributed significantly to the miscalculation.

The engineer who told this story said he knew of it because he worked for NASA then and was assigned to simulate the effect of waste and water dumps on flight trajectories.

"Fortunately, I didn't have to work with any real data," he said.

Back on earth, secret government message traffic caused snafus in the civilian arena. Top-secret computer communications during President Ronald Reagan's tenure exasperated ordinary joes who simply wanted to park their cars. Whenever Reagan's airborne command plane, the modified Boeing 747, parked at March Air Force Base during one of his numerous vacations while in office, thousands of remote-control garage door openers in the San Bernardino area went wiggy and refused to work. March Air Force Base is about ten miles south of San Bernardino.

Residents accused the president's entourage of jamming the neighborhood's electric garage door openers, because the trouble began when Reagan visited his nearby Santa Barbara mountaintop ranch and ended when he flew away in the command post. The owner of an electronic garage door opener company in San Bernardino said he was sure high-powered radio transmissions from the president's airborne command post jammed signals of the garage door openers' remote-control switches, adding that he'd had eight- or nine hundred complaints about operating failures in less than a week when Reagan arrived to vacation. The company owner said a communications satellite sending scrambled signals apparently bombarded the garage door openers in their 300-megahertz operating range, crippling them.

Of course, automatic door openers that swoon over *Air Force One* are not significant problems. However, even a small glitch could have serious consequences in the nation's computerized missile defense system. Take these examples:

- On June 3, 1980, a faulty chip triggered alarms in the underground Omaha post of the Strategic Air Command. Screens lit up showing two Russian missiles attacking from the North Atlantic. B-52 crews prepared for takeoff, but when headquarters checked with radar stations, the stations reported no missiles. For almost four minutes, the United States was preparing to go to war because of a defective computer chip.

- On November 9, 1979, a military worker accidentally fed a training tape into the North American Aerospace Defense Command's computers, making it look as if the United States were undergoing a multiple missile attack.

- On July 22, 1962, NASA destroyed a mission in flight when it blew up the *Mariner 1* Venus probe because its combined Atlas and Agena missiles went out of control, endangering human lives and shipping lanes. Seventy-six tense seconds after the trouble began, a range officer destroyed the missile just before the Atlas and Agena missile separation would have made destruction impossible. A minor error in the computer's missile guidance program made the $18,500,000 rocket lose control. A single character missing from that program—something like a bar over the letter *R*, or a hyphen—caused flawed signals that sent it veering.

- October 5, 1960, almost became the last date in history when an iceberg nearly helped trigger World War III. One civilian witness who lived a lifetime of fear in just a few minutes later recalled what became known as the famous Thule incident.

Computer businessmen visiting the North American Air Defense Command (NORAD) headquarters in Colorado Springs, Colorado, had just been told that a panel they were examining, which had five lights, lit up in increasing order of the possibility of an air attack.

"As I recall it," said Peter G. Peterson, executive vice-president of Bell and Howell, "We were told that if No. 1 flashed, it meant only routine objects were in the air. If No. 2 flashed, it meant a few more unidentified objects, but nothing suspicious. If No. 5 flashed, it was highly probable that objects in a raid were moving toward America."

The panel lights rapidly lit up: No. 1, No. 2, No. 3.

"When the number rose to 4," Peterson said, "key NORAD generals came running from their offices. Then the number rose to 5."

Peterson and the other executives were rushed into an office to endure twenty minutes of "absolute terror." The Ballistic Missile Early-Warning System in Thule, Greenland, had picked up signals the computer analyzed as missiles flying from Russia to the United States. Strategic Air Command headquarters in Nebraska went on alert as SAC crews all over the world prepared to scramble.

Canadian Air Marshal C. Roy Slemon finally contacted Greenland personnel, who reported that their warning system wasn't working properly but that they couldn't contact NORAD, because an iceberg had cut their submarine cable link. The "missiles" that the warning system's radar picked up turned out to be—the moon. The radar had bounced off the moon, divided the moon's distance from the earth by 3,000 miles, and reported the 2,200 miles left over as the distance from which the "missiles" were coming.

One person is so concerned about the rush to judgment from warning to nuclear response that he is suing the U.S. military and may take his case to the Supreme Court. The computer manager Cliff Johnson of Stanford University believes that the Pentagon is breaking the law with its automated Launch on Warning system. The system can scramble jets carrying nuclear warheads in under five minutes if computers determine from radar and satellites that a nuclear attack is coming. The jets could launch their missiles within ten minutes of takeoff, while underground silos could launch theirs even faster.

Johnson, a British citizen, says he thought of the lawsuit after the military "put a missile in London," his hometown. His argument is that only Congress has the right to declare war, a right the computer usurps. He believes the Launch on Warning System doesn't give anyone time to determine whether a computer bug is giving a false reading.

"You can't have a safe decision in less time than it takes to have a cup of tea," he said in a May 1989 *ComputerWorld* interview after filing suit against the Strategic Air Command, adding that if he lost, he'd appeal to the U.S. Supreme Court.

Perhaps the specter of Armageddon is what draws hackers who feel compelled to break into "secure" systems. Or, perhaps it's merely the thrill of sneaking into a place where you are forbidden to go. For many computer aficionados, breaking security is half the excitement of having a computer.

The fascination with security was reflected at MIT years ago in hacker-devised programs with names like "J. Edgar Hoover," "Spy," or "Fido." In Fido, the operator tells the program to let him know when So-and-so logs on. Fido will sniff around the system until that person appears, then inform its master. Spy allows the operator to look at everything that his chosen target prints. J. Edgar Hoover tells the operator if someone is spying on him and can "gun down" the interloper by logging him off.

One MIT story from about twenty years ago throws a boomerang at the "Unclassified," "Classified," and "Secret" security clearances the Pentagon used. The Pentagon had a three-tiered computer system where messages could be sent from the bottom up, but not from the top down. At the bottom was the Unclassified user, who could send messages to anyone at his level or higher. Next was the Classified user, who could send a message to anyone at *his* level or higher, but in order to prevent him from spilling the beans on the latest weapon of mass destruction, he could not send messages down to Unclassified. At the top was the Secret user, who could communicate with other Secret users, with the Cabots, or with God, but not with anyone lower down.

An Unclassified worker tried a trick named Amyl Fax Shuffle Time, which sounds like a popular dance from the Roaring Twenties but is actually a program that works like an electronic boomerang. Amyl Fax Shuffle Time is a time delay program in which the perpetrator invents a message, adds his target's name to it, and sends it on its way. A while later the message returns and pops up on the perpetrator's screen, looking for all the world as if it came from his target. The trick's only purpose is humor; for instance, you can send out a "message" in which your target accuses you of having a face like a Moon Pie, then present the "evidence" and demand that he or she apologize, generating mirth as that person squirms in confusion.

The Unclassified user had a friend on the Secret level, so he threw the boomerang at him and wandered off. In his absence, a general passed by his screen, looked, and froze in shock. An insulting message from a Secret user had broken the security system and ended up on an Unclassified screen! Furious at the security breach, Pentagon officials supposedly were on the verge of suing the security system's designer before they discovered it was a joke.

Divine inspiration launched another security scare at a large Florida Air Force base. A colonel there who wrote a term paper at home for a war college correspondence course used the base's VAX mainframe to print it out. He was scanning through the hard copy when REPENT AND BE SAVED! leaped out at him. He quickly flipped through the pages to find more warnings: JESUS CHRIST IS COMING TODAY! HAVE YOU GIVEN YOURSELF TO THE LORD?

This looked like a major security breach at a base that did a great deal of classified research. He called the commanding general, who called the head of the computer center, and the three started their hunt for the revivalist ghost.

They ran through every nook and cranny of the VAX, finding nothing. A week later, a worker at the computer center asked the colonel to bring in the program from his home computer that he'd used to communicate with the VAX. It was a shareware program that the worker had, in fact, given to the colonel in the first place. The worker snooped through the disk, and sure enough, hidden in it was a communication program chock-full of gospel sayings. Their prayers had been answered—the military mainframe was still secure.

Diddling around with a classified computer system is one way to let off steam; whether it's fun or criminal depends on your point of view and on what system's broken into. Whenever he gets mad at his boss, one legendary computer expert at the Pentagon plays with the computer so that his boss can't determine the army's troop strength to within 300,000 men, give or take a decimal point.

Not surprisingly, generals are often the butt of computer jokes in the military. A sad sack who may have related to a computer as a fellow dogface, subject to the whims and barks of generals, probably made up this one:

Researchers finally completed a powerful computer for use in long-term planning by the Pentagon. A five-star general had the honor of asking it its first question. Aware he was onstage, the general, in one of those madcap moments to which generals are prone, told the clerk to ask the machine, "Will it be peace or war?"

The clerk typed in the query, and the machine answered YES.

Annoyed, the general shouted, "Yes, WHAT?!"

The machine replied YES, *SIR*.

Another Pentagon story concerns MIT hackers in the early days of telephone hacking. The hackers used a powerful PDP-1 mainframe to connect with the MIT telephone extension system. From that, they compiled lists of "tie lines"—other telephone lines that tied into the system.

From there, they were able to "travel" from Lincoln Labs to Bell Labs, the SAC system, and the Pentagon. They programmed the mainframe to call up numbers consecutively, noting which combinations made a telephone ring and which ones were duds. They were discovered only because the Pentagon telephones were also arranged sequentially, so that as the computer tested the numbers, the phone rang once in an office, then once in the adjoining office, and so on, rippling down the hall. Ever-vigilant members of our nation's armed forces grew suspicious. A few days later, the mischievous hackers looked up from their telephone number spreadsheet to see Pentagon officials standing in the doorway, and they weren't smiling.

Telephone hackers, called phone phreaks, are drawn to secure systems like squirrels to walnut trees, eager to crack the shell that protects the sweet treasure within. Their curiosity resembles that of a ten-year-old encountering a large multilegged insect. Boy, the ten-year-old thinks, that sure is ugly. I wonder what would happen if I touched it. I wonder what would happen if I dropped this brick on it.

The spiritual grandfather of all phone phreaks is John Draper, alias Captain Crunch, who did time alongside second-story men for breaking into the telephone company's long-distance lines and making free calls back in the early 1970s. Draper's nickname came from his serendipitous discovery that the free whistles in boxes of Cap'n Crunch cereal had exactly the same frequency the telephone company used to connect lines with long-distance circuits. Blow the whistle into the telephone, and the AT&T computer would automatically transfer one's line to a long-distance trunk for free.

Draper also built blue boxes, compulsively working on ways to break into the telephone system. A "blue box" is a device that lets the user make long-distance calls for free by imitating the telephone company's computerized access beeps that switch callers over to long-distance lines. Draper was convicted and put on probation for one blue-box escapade, then tossed into jail for another. Apple Corporation hired him after he served his time, unaware that Draper remained entranced by the music of the AT&T spheres. He immediately designed a telephone interface board that was also a blue box, but the company axed his project before he had a chance to send thousands of blue boxes into production.

Another felonious hacker, who is now a consultant, is Ian A. Murphy of Philadelphia, a.k.a. Captain Zap. As a lad, Murphy liked to tap into his neighbors' telephone lines. He advanced to tapping into academic records, credit ratings, and a Pentagon list of missile sites targeted at America. He ended up as the self-confessed leader of a group that ran up $212,000 in telephone bills by means of a blue box. His group also swiped

$200,000 in hardware by charging it to stolen credit card numbers. The government got hacked off enough to put Murphy in jail.

After he was sprung, Murphy couldn't find a job in computers, so he switched from hacker to hack—he became a cabbie. On his day of destiny, a manager for the Dun & Bradstreet Corporation stepped into his cab when Murphy just happened to have a printout of instructions for breaking into Dun & Bradstreet's system. Murphy showed him the printout and nailed his first client. He now reportedly charges $800 a day to cruise electronic bulletin boards looking for hackers trying to break into his clients' computers, or tries to break into the systems himself to show customers how to improve security.

At least one other hacker with dreams of fat consultant fees used his home computer to reach out from the Kansas plains and touch the U.S. Air Force in a sensitive place. A fourteen-year-old hacker from Prairie Village, Kansas, wanted to persuade companies to hire him as a computer security consultant, so he broke into the confidential files of about two hundred commercial companies as well as the unclassified Air Force satellite-positioning system. The *Kansas City Star* reported in 1989 that, rather than persuading companies to hire him, the boy was visited by military and company investigators who persuaded *him* to show them how he broke into their systems.

Public sophistication about phone phreaks, modems, and so forth has improved. In one story from ancient times when many people didn't know what a "computer" was, the MIT university computer system would automatically call other systems to exchange mail. One line started to fail consistently. No one could figure out why. A programmer decided to monitor the calls when the line went on. The line activated, the computer placed a call, and the call was answered at the other end. The computer let out a shrill tone to indicate it was ready to transmit information, and its shriek was met with silence. Then a voice at the answering end said, "Hey Martha, it's the nut with the whistle again," and hung up.

We've come a long way. Today's sophisticated telephone answerer would probably respond, "Hey Martha, it's that nut with the modem again. He thinks we're a mainframe," and *then* hang up.

People are now so knowledgeable about computers that even unfortunate fellows who lack the talents of a Captain Crunch might know how to pull a few electronic strings when they're in a jam, as happened in 1984 in California's Santa Clara County. A prison inmate somehow broke into the on-line prison information system and changed his release date from December 31 to December 5. A deputy got suspicious and caught the change when he compared computer dates to manual records. The inmate said he made the change because he wanted to be home for Christmas.

Those whose computer crimes are especially malicious or destructive are technoterrorists, phantoms who steal without leaving fingerprints and terrorize without guns. Unlike CREEP's gang of dirty tricksters during Watergate, technoterrorists don't tape open door locks when they burglarize offices, so it takes more than an alert janitor to discover them. Apparently, some technoterrorists have found their niche in the shadier recesses of American politics, picking up where old-fashioned burglars left off.

In March 1986, a member of the staff of California Representative Ed Zschau, Republican, was working late when a beep told her someone had entered the computer system from an outside telephone line. Her computer screen went blank. When the system came back on, more than two hundred letters and information on mailing addresses had disappeared from the computer file. Four days later, staff workers of another Republican, Representative John McCain of Arizona, reported that someone using an outside telephone line reached into

McCain's computer and destroyed hundreds of letters and mailing addresses during the lunch hour.

Both Zschau and McCain were running for Senate seats at the time. It was, Zschau said, "tantamount to someone breaking into my office, taking my files and burning them." He added, "The police would be more concerned if this were a physical break-in. . . . Because people don't see the files overturned or a pile of ashes outside the door, it doesn't seem as bad. . . . But it is equally as devastating. . . . Every office in Capitol Hill can be broken into in this way and the files deleted."

Human nature makes many computer systems remarkably easy to crack. The congressmen's computer systems might have been more secure than most—an executive for a company selling computer equipment on Capitol Hill said the break-in would require the expertise of "someone really sophisticated, with a Ph.D. in math or computer science"—but many systems are poorly secured. People with loose lips drop passwords that get overheard, use passwords easily guessed by others, or grow lax about security measures because, after all, the system wasn't broken into last year, last month, yesterday, or today, so it won't be broken into tomorrow.

A British newspaper noted how easy it is for English techno-terrorists to get into systems. It reported that the culprits were usually not teenage computer wizards but disgruntled employees and previous employees. The insurance brokerage firm Hogg Robinson released an audit of fifty firms that showed how carelessly companies choose passwords. Auditors of all but three firms surveyed unsuccessfully used passwords to prevent unauthorized access to their computers, defeated by their own predictability in choosing passwords. People often used names of spouses or pets, easy choices for others to guess. America's favorite password was "love," closely followed by "sex." The favorite password in Britain was "Fred," another indication that the British are an inscrutable and peculiar race. Other favorites were "God" and "hacker," though some fools preferred "genius" and some decided that "pass" was too sneaky to pass up. A Hogg Robinson representative said a hacker trying those passwords would get through 20 percent of the time.

Even those cynical boys in blue might let down their guard when showing off their computer system to tykes from the local school, unaware that one of those cute kids has a computer in his basement and a good memory for passwords. In one story, a Philadelphia boy went on a field trip to the local police station, where the cops showed off their computerized criminal files. He was so tickled by the fact that the officers made no effort to hide their passwords and access techniques that he went home to his personal computer and broke into the criminal files, entering his teachers for crimes such as "intellectual murder." A friendly man from the FBI visited him a few days later and told him not to do it again.

That boy, clever though he was, would have to take a backseat to one of the cleverest espionage hoaxes in the last decade. Strictly speaking, it wasn't a hack, merely an elaborate joke, but it threw Usenet computer fans into tizzies, convincing some that the KGB had tapped their net.

The April 1, 1984, message appeared to originate from the Kremlin by a user named Chernenko (the name of the Soviet Union's current prime minister). It went like this:

> Well, today, 840401, this is at last the Socialist Union of Soviet Republics joining the Usenet network and saying hallo to everybody.
>
> One reason for us to join this network has been to have a means of having an open discussion forum with the American and European people and making clear to them our strong efforts towards attaining peaceful coexistence between the people of the Soviet Union and those of the United States and Europe.

We have been informed that on this network many people have given strong anti-Russian opinions, but we believe they have been misguided by their leaders, especially the American administration, who is seeking for war and domination of the world. By well informing those people from our side we hope to have a possibility to make clear to them our intentions and ideas.

Some of those in the Western world, who believe in the truth of what we say have made possible our entry on this network; to them we are very grateful. We hereby invite you to freely give your comments and opinions.

The user then gave a return address at the Kremlin, care of the KGB, and concluded, "And now, let's open a flask of Vodka and have a drink on our entry on this network. So: NA ZDAROVJE!"

Two weeks later, Piet Beertema of Amsterdam sent this message out on Usenet: "Thanks to all of you, netpals, who replied to my 'USSR on Usenet' article. Reading all your replies really made worth while the forging I had to do to hide the real origin. . . . 'Sorry' for those who took this April Fool so bloody serious. . . . (I got serious letters more than 3 pages long!)."

Among the responses Beertema received were the following:

Welcome! [From an isolated CIA outpost]
Is this for real? Can we have confirmation from someone who is recognized as being in a position to know?
I knew there was a path to the Russians on the net! Now at last we can exchange netnews messages about high school reunions and our latest cryptoanalytic results. Thank you eversomuch.

'Bobby... have you been playing with those access codes again?'

MONEY
MONEY
MONEY

He was just another lonely account manager lost in the shuffle, spending his life keeping his desk neat and going home to feed the cat. But he had a dream. He realized in his simple banker's way that if he had a million dollars, his life would not be so boring, and he could even get another cat. But how? How could he get a million dollars? If only . . .

One day, the lowly manager made an interesting discovery. Roving through the computer, he noticed that whenever the bank rounded off the fractions of a penny from the interest accumulated on accounts, it did so in the bank's favor. The manager knew that a penny saved is a penny earned, and that with hundreds of thousands of pennies saved from client accounts every day, the bank was making a tidy bundle. Thinking it a shame that all this money went to a heartless institution that couldn't enjoy it, the manager created a fake account for himself under the alias Joe Zzwick and told the computer to take all those penny fractions and deposit them in the last account in the alphabetical file.

Thousands of dollars a week rolled into the Zzwick account. The manager made a few withdrawals, but tried to keep his life simple. He got another cat. He bought nicer cat food. He traded in his Ford Fairmont for a Porsche (banker's gray, of course) and bought a condo in the city where he spent weekends with a bar hostess named Candi. Monday through Friday he was Harry in accounting, but Friday night to Monday morning he was Crazy Joe, the hottest dancer at the Rio.

Alas, the world was cruel to Harry and his dream. About a year later, the bank's advertising agency decided on a new campaign with the slogan "We serve your needs from A to Z." For it, they planned to contact the first and last people on the account list and use them in the commercials. But wait, this guy Zzwick's account is as curious as his name. All these strange deposits and withdrawals . . .

It was curtains for Harry. He lost his condo, his girl, his banker's gray Porsche. He didn't lose his newfound talent for dancing, but it's not a skill much in demand at the federal penitentiary.

This story has as many versions as a preacher has sermons on greed. Adrian Norman's book *Computer Insecurity* lists two, one of which appeared in the British magazine *Computer Digest* in July 1975. Perhaps the story is popular not only because it's unusual (how many ad men solve criminal acts instead of committing them?) but because we can identify with mousy, downtrodden Harry, within whose timid heart beats the savage rhythm of Crazy Joe. The secret is money. We fantasize that, with money, we will be transformed from everyday *shlumps* into rich, well-tanned, well-traveled, adored, polo-playing, bon-mot-uttering *shlumps*. It's something to dream about.

Maybe the glow of riches is what makes the "lobby deposit slip heist" as popular as the Zzwick tale despite holes in the story that you could drive a steamer through. The story's about an ordinary guy who, by knowing a little bit about computers, makes an extraordinary pile of money.

In the tale, the man goes into the bank lobby and swipes a

sheaf of generic deposit slips that the bank keeps there for the convenience of customers who left their personal deposit slips at home. He takes them home and writes his account number at the bottom of each slip in invisible magnetic ink. No human eye can read it, but a computer can, and it will mistake the slips for personal slips marked in (visible) magnetic ink, the kind of slips that the computer's programmed to automatically deposit into the given account number.

He returns to the bank and surreptitiously puts the altered slips on the lobby table. Normally, the bank computer would take a generic deposit slip and boot it out for a human teller to read, since it isn't marked with magnetic ink, but the altered slips mean that people who use them for a deposit are unwittingly putting their hard-earned money into the sly fox's account.

The man visits the bank a few weeks later with a briefcase handcuffed to his wrist, and inquires about his account, which now contains a fortune. He tells the manager that he needs cash and is closing the account, walking out the door with a bulging briefcase. Soon thereafter, customers getting their balance statements discover that their deposits aren't going into their accounts. By the time investigators figure out what went on, the thief is sipping mimosas on the beach of a tropical island with difficult extradition laws.

The computer unleashes scores of novel ways to embezzle, a rather ironic potential, considering the antimaterialistic philosophy of many hackers during the sixties and early seventies. Creating ways to free the masses from confusion and drudgery by designing ever-better computers and software was a noble undertaking; expecting cash in return was vulgar. In the best of all possible worlds, a software designer would post his work on an electronic bulletin board and let others copy it for free, asking only that anyone who really liked the program send him five dollars or so to help him buy the freedom to design new programs. Apparently, this system worked at the beginning, even when the occasional jerk stole someone's free software and marketed it for profit.

Independent software designers felt proud of the difference between themselves and the money-grubbing computer giants who plastered their software packages with legal maledictions. One Canadian software firm lampoons the big companies' paranoia about protecting copyrights with its "Bloodthirsty License Agreement," whose humor and trust in its clients' honesty reflects the increasingly rare hacker spirit:

"Bloodthirsty License Agreement"

This is where the bloodthirsty license agreement is supposed to go, explaining that EasyFlow is a copyrighted package, sternly warning you not to pirate copies of it and explaining, in detail, the gory consequences if you do.

We know that you are an honest person, and are not going to go around pirating copies of EasyFlow; this is just as well with us since we worked hard to perfect it and selling copies of it is our only method of making anything out of all the hard work.

If, on the other hand, you are one of those few people who do go around pirating copies of software you probably aren't going to pay much attention to a license agreement, bloodthirsty or not. Just keep your doors locked and look out for the HavenTree attack shark.

"Honest Disclaimer"

We don't claim EasyFlow is good for anything—if you think it is, great, but it's up to you to decide. If EasyFlow doesn't work: tough. If you lose a million because EasyFlow messes up, it's you that's out the million, not us. If you don't like this disclaimer: tough. We reserve the right to do the absolute minimum provided by law, up to and including nothing.

This is basically the same disclaimer that comes with all

software packages, but ours is in plain English and theirs is in legalese.

We don't really want to include any disclaimer at all, but our lawyers insisted. We tried to ignore them but they threatened us with the attack shark (see license agreement above) at which point we relented.

Independent computer experts were also nauseated by the unsavory methods some firms used to squeeze more bucks out of customers, such as making minor changes in mainframes that vastly increase their operating speeds, then charging a fortune for the improvement. Some firms were said to make minor changes that even *slowed down* a system so that they could sell that computer for one price and its faster twin for much more. Stories flourish of how IBM, or the Burroughs Corporation, or General Electric, or some other heavyweight would sell two mainframes at widely different prices even though the machines were identical but for a minor, easily remedied difference. The companies would charge steep fees to upgrade the slow machine, the upgrading consisting of nothing more than the addition or removal of a circuit board, wire, or internal clock.

One user, aware that a company charged thousands of dollars for an upgrading that merely required removing a single wire from the machine, supposedly printed the following memo on that company's letterhead and mailed it out to the firm's customers:

CAUTION: Do not remove the wire from pin 4AB to 7FL in the CPU enclosure. This wire is located approximately seven inches up from the bottom of the backplane in Bay 2 and should not be removed by using a 112-3 wire unwrapping tool, first not removing the wrapping from 4AB, then not pulling the wire from under the other wiring to its bound end at 7FL, followed by not unwrapping the bound end from 7FL. Not removing this wire will result in the normal clock speed, which is 1.6 times slower than with the wire removed and will not cause corresponding increases in system throughput.

As the year 2000 draws nigh, most computer experts have lost their youthful weakness for generosity. Hackers and phone phreaks have dropped the altruistic mores of groups such as California's now-defunct Homebrew Computer Club, whose members swapped parts and expertise for free and honestly believed that the liberation of the people would be achieved when everyone had a personal computer. The pressures of making enough to live on were too much for the flower children of the Age of Aquarius. The lure of making more than enough to live by committing an illegality here and there sucked in a few kids who might otherwise have followed in their forebears' sandal steps.

One former kid sent to dangle slowly, slowly in the wind of the penal system was Herbert Zinn, Jr., of Chicago, alias Shadow Hawk. In 1987, this high school dropout broke into the computer systems of NATO, the Defense Department, and AT&T. He stole $1.2 million in software by downloading it into his personal computer at a time when he was not even old enough to vote. He then published the systems' passwords on computer bulletin boards.

His three-month adventure ended with his arrest. In January 1989, Zinn had the dubious honor of being one of the first hackers in the nation to be convicted under the Computer Fraud and Abuse Act of 1986. A federal judge sentenced him to nine months in prison, a $10,000 fine, and thirty months' probation, emphasizing that Zinn, and not his parents, was responsible for paying the fine.

Another hacker venturing beyond the pale of the law fared better than Zinn when he was caught only because regulations for prosecuting computer theft were still being defined. Jerry Neal Schneider started a telephone and electronics equipment sales company by impersonating a journalist on a visit to Pacific Telephone and Telegraph's supply office. He observed how employees used a special telephone to enter equipment orders in code.

He went out and got a similar telephone, broke the company's codes, and used them to divert PT&T equipment to a central warehouse, where he picked the equipment up in a used PT&T truck he'd bought at an auction. He made off with a million dollars worth of material before being caught. Schneider served forty days in a minimum-security prison, paid a $500 fine, and became a computer security consultant.

The use of "blue boxes" was not the only way to hoodwink Ma Bell. One computer expert recalled a friend of his who lived in New Jersey. During the 1970s, New Jersey Bell apparently sent keypunch cards out with its bills. The friend took the phone bill card to a keypunch at work and added an overpunch to the bill amount, making it a negative number. He sent in a check for the regular amount along with the altered card; his next month's bill listed credit for his payment, plus a credit that strangely materialized from his previous balance due.

Another phone phreak story involves electronic skulduggery worthy of the CIA. It's about a hacker who discovers that the micro minicomputer that runs an automatic teller machine, or ATM, is linked by telephone to the main office computer. Whenever someone requests a withdrawal, the micro minicomputer contacts the main computer by means of an easily cracked communication code and asks it to check the request.

The hacker taps into the telephone line with a monitor that breaks the connection if the minicomputer has a question about *his* account. Mimicking the main office computer, the monitor gives the man permission to withdraw any amount, so he cleans out all the cash dispensers. He's caught only when telephone maintenance workers discover the tap.

Money can be a currency of revenge as well as purchase. In one rather baroque tale, a fired employee didn't just leave his name secreted in the computer's payroll program but also gave himself a pay raise and racked up $10 million. Unsure what to do with the money and reluctant to get arrested on suspicion of drug dealing by depositing it in a U.S. bank, he wired the loot to Europe, then went there himself and bought $10 million worth of diamonds. He then hired a lawyer to help him figure out what to do with his rocks, but the snitch contacted the FBI.

This story may take its plot from a $10 million embezzlement carried out in 1978. R., a systems analyst, impersonated a bank official and visited the wire transfer room at the Security Pacific Bank in Los Angeles, where he observed how transfers were made, and transferred about $10 million to his account at New York's Irving Trust Company. He then sent some of those funds to Russalmaz, the USSR's official diamond broker, buying about $8 million of diamonds. R. tried to sell some of the diamonds in Beverly Hills, California, before the FBI arrested him and charged him with wire fraud, smuggling, interstate transportation of stolen property, and entering a bank to commit a felony. R. pled guilty to wire fraud in return for having the other charges dropped. While out on bond, he and an accomplice were arrested for taking another stab at wire fraud in a similar scheme.

Naturally, looting a system is easier if you're already on the inside. In a true-life scandal, the chief teller for a New York bank embezzled $1.5 million by creating a computer program that transferred money from other accounts into his, transferring it back when interest payments were being determined so that he wouldn't be detected. He was caught not by bank employees but by cops after his bookie was raided. He'd been embezzling for three years.

The teller later told his story in an issue of *Bank Systems and*

Equipment. "You might think that it made up a legendary king's ransom and that I would have coffers full of money," he said. "But I do not. To me, every dollar was another link in the chains of an all-too-real nightmare. I am a compulsive gambler. Every cent I took from the bank went to support my habit. . . . When the police told officers at the bank that I was betting and often losing $30,000 a day, they were reluctant to believe it. But the facts are irrefutable."

He related how he started the same way other tellers began lives of theft, by simply taking cash from his register. Because he was a supervisor, he moved on to the more sophisticated method of stealing from large accounts via the computer. If that money might be missed, he'd steal money from another account and put it into the first, adjusting the computer record. But this meant that he was trapped within his own pyramid scheme, constantly having to pay off embezzled accounts by stealing from others. When he was caught, he was juggling more than fifty accounts.

"This worked, but near the end my hands were trembling," he said.

An insider working with other insiders to loot the system can haul in amounts that make a few million look like cab fare. Take what was probably the biggest insurance scam in the last forty years, the Equity Funding Corporation scandal. From 1964 to 1972, top management at the Equity Funding Corporation of America exaggerated company earnings in order to buy assets and obtain loans. The managers also fed their computer thousands of bogus "customers," selling their policies to underwriters. The swindle cost insurance clients a billion dollars in lost policies, and shareholders $600 million in lost stock, and resulted in twenty-two fraud convictions.

For every embezzlement tale that lands in the newspapers, many more never see the light of publicity. One computer expert who was in a bank's service bureau recalled the unreported scheme of a bank programmer who wrote a program that dumped out a list of all the dormant accounts. The programmer put in his home address as a change of address for one of the accounts once or twice a week, then cashed a check for the account's balance. Once it cleared and he got the canceled check in the mail, he'd change the account's address back to what it had been, and nobody was the wiser. He was caught only because a key entry operator made an error that caused one of the checks to bounce. The bounced check was examined by someone in another department who looked up where the check writer lived.

The programmer absconded with about $40,000. The bank made him agree to pay it back, and management put his name on the blacklist for banks. That was all the bank did, keeping it quiet in order to avoid a scandal.

Even lowly clerks can get into the act. A clerk in a possibly apocryphal story found that, the Grateful Dead song notwithstanding, it's pretty easy to run with the weight of gold. He'd been working in a bank's computer division less than a year when he sent a computer message to the Brink's depository that stored and handled the bank's gold bullion. The message ordered Brink's to send forty-four kilos of gold to a post office box in a small California town. Brink's sent the gold bars to the address, where the employee or a confederate picked it up. The employee then disappeared and was never found. The bank, now that the horse was out of the barn, checked his previous employment references and discovered they were phony.

Sometimes a computer inadvertently opens the curtain on a small morality play about theft, understanding, and human nature, as in the mom-and-pop grocery store mystery, in which a firm that installed a computer at the store to balance the books found a consistent error that puzzled everyone. About thirty dollars was missing from the account balance every month. The firm sent people to nail down the glitch responsible for the mistake, but to no avail. What should have been a minor computer bug blew up into a major headache as dozens of the firm's representatives visited the store, determined to get to the bottom of the matter, only to be frustrated.

They finally went to the store owner and said, "We don't know where the money is going." The owner asked how much it was, and they told him. He said, "Oh, that's fine, I know exactly where it is. One of my employees is stealing it." The representatives wanted to call the cops, but the owner told them to back off, saying, "The clerk stealing the money is worth it, but if I gave it to him then I'd have to give everybody else a raise, so I want to keep it just the way it is."

Money, computers, and local culture clashed in another mystery in the Virginia hills at a garment-sewing factory. The factory had computer readers at every table to record how much piecework was done by the seamstresses, almost all of whom were women.

On payroll day, the more they sewed, the more they earned, and the computer readers tended to increase productivity since the workers could see from them how they were doing. But about an hour and a half before the end of their shift, some employees' productivity would fall way off, more than could be expected to happen from fatigue.

The computer consultants asked around and found that some women were monitoring their pay. When they got to the point where they'd bring home more money than their husbands, they stopped working. They didn't want to out-earn their husbands, because of the social stigma attached to it, the insult to their husbands' status. The factory managers started allowing workers to take time off with pay and also gave them credit at the company store so that at Christmastime they could spend the fruits of their extra productivity on presents.

Incidents on the small scale of a mom-and-pop grocery or a backwoods town sound quaint. Such minor financial slips are easy to remedy. But when the Federal Reserve's computers slip up, it's like an elephant slipping on a banana peel—the crash brings an earthquake felt for miles. In January 1986, the federal government accidentally transferred $2 billion to nineteen financial institutions.

A weekend computer test that federal workers ran by using old copies of 1,000 previous transactions was left lying around. Someone picked the test up the following Monday and mistakenly ran it on the wire as the real thing, depositing $2 billion into private company coffers. A spokesman for the Federal Reserve made a point of saying that the $2 billion transferred was only 2 percent of the funds handled every day by the federal government, as if to comfort the spooked financial community by assuring it that the Fed had money to burn. All the money was recovered, and six employees were suspended three days without pay. The Fed made sure that such mistakes wouldn't happen again by using fake transactions and special account numbers for tests.

A billion dollars is a big enough number to make even bankers emotional. In 1985, the Bank of New York—one of the twenty largest in the United States—incurred a $32 billion overdraft at its cash account with the New York Federal Reserve Bank when a computer failure snarled thousands of government securities transactions. Working furiously to race the clock, they reduced the overdraft to a mere $24 billion by day's end. The bank had to borrow that amount from the New York Federal Reserve, pledging all of its assets in return, just to balance its accounts overnight.

When it comes to money, computers can be just as screwy as people. However, a sense of righteousness rather than rapaciousness seems to drive them. One of the tales you might hear at a party goes like this: A woman gets a bill from her credit card company for zero dollars and zero cents. She laughs and tosses it in the trash. Two weeks later she gets another bill from the company for zero dollars and zero cents, with a computerized form letter urging her to pay up. She shrugs and tosses that. Two weeks pass and she gets the same bill for $0.00, with a nasty form letter telling her her credit will be ruined if she doesn't pay up. So she writes out a check for zero dollars and zero cents, sends it in, and never hears from the computer again.

"This happened to me with a medical bill," wrote Bret Jolly of UCLA. "I used to have the bill posted up in my office at work. The folks at the billing company were appropriately chagrined when I told them." Another person wrote, "I actually had a firm send me a computerized bill for zero dollars. After about four months of getting this bill, I sent a quote to this business for the time it would take to solve their zero dollar billing problem. It was then that they realized the problem and had someone else solve it."

Computers can also be generous about giving zero dollars to employees who have earned them.

"My father worked as a lecturer for Washington University," noted Mark Robert Smith of Rutgers University. "This was in the old days when paychecks were punched and typed on IBM cards. One pay period, the computer got confused and thought that he was underpaid by $0.00. So it kept reporting him as underpaid, asking for authorization from the operator to pay him. The operator tried for six consecutive months to clear the error, but was unable to, so my father received a check for $0.00 and the error was cleared. He still has the check."

A computer tried to give away millions of dollars in October 1988 in Kansas City. The DeVry Institute of Technology student Neil Martin received two unsolicited money machine cards in the mail for accounts at Home Savings, which was merging with Safety Federal Savings and Loan and starting a new computer system.

He tried one, ironically named Safecard, at an automatic

teller. The screen told him he had $999,999.99 available for withdrawal. He tried the second card. It also said he had $999,999.99.

Some of us might have gotten slaphappy and acted capriciously, if illegally. Not so this upstanding lad. He went home and slept on his good fortune, then returned the next day and withdrew $10 from each account. His balance didn't change. He contacted the savings and loan, which told him he wasn't the only instant millionaire in town.

Computers can be freewheeling about giving money away, but shy about receiving it. In fact, they can be more than shy—they can be downright apoplectic. Bob Knighten, a Massachusetts computer professional, related a story of a friend's zero-sum voyage into conceptual art, an adventure her bank didn't appreciate:

Phyllis sent two of her children to spend a week with a friend, Mary, living in New York's Greenwich Village. Mary squired the kids around, taking them to museums, Broadway shows, concerts, and other tourist attractions. She carefully kept track of what she spent on the kids. At the end of the week, the kids went back home and Mary prepared an itemized invoice with charges for all of the kids' activities. Offsetting this was credit for amusement, love, laughs, and so on. The net charge was $0.00.

Mary sent the invoice to Phyllis. Phyllis was amused and asked Mary if she could also have Mary's receipts, because she wanted to make much of this into a collage. To go with the invoice, she sent a check to Mary for $0.00 with the request that Mary deposit the check so that Phyllis could get it back with the usual bank markings on it. Mary promptly deposited her check, and it even showed up as credit for $0.00 on her next statement.

Two months later, Phyllis still had not gotten her check back. She finally called her bank and, after some run-around, spoke to a vice-president. He snarled back that the check for

$0.00 had caused the bank's accounting program to core dump! This cost the bank many thousands of dollars, and he was *not* amused. Phyllis never got her check back, but she made the collage anyway.

The streak of altruism running through the veins of ancient software designers still seems to course through the circuits of their creations, computers now stuck in ATMs doling out greenbacks to housewives, executives, and impecunious students. Those computers must often regret their lost opportunities to be music synthesizers or sonar trackers for Jacques Cousteau, to do something exciting. Why not forget this doling-out bit and go wild, making people happy by flooding them with dollar bills?

Several years ago an ATM did just that. It used a clip dispenser to hand out $25 a shot, and a customer discovered he could empty the machine by pushing the clip back into its slot. The machine would send another $25 out and keep doing so as long as the clip was pushed back in and it had cash in its bin. He emptied the machine of several thousand dollars, put it all in a paper bag, and left.

The next day, the man went to the bank's main office and told its manager, "Your teller machines can be robbed." The manager sputtered and denied this, of course, so the man dumped a bag of cash on the desk and responded, "You won't be wanting this back, then."

The bank's ATMs were down for several days.

More recently, sixteen ATMs throughout the Washington, D.C., area gave a man with a stolen VISA card $140,000 in ten- and twenty-dollar bills. The man confessed in federal court that he used the stolen credit card to make more than four hundred withdrawals during a crisp October weekend.

"Why didn't someone else in line notice it?" asked the Secret Service agent John Magaw. "It's very bizarre. All of a sudden this guy realized how good he had it. His pockets just weren't big enough. The machines just weren't programmed to stop." ATM monitors photographed the man pulling out $300 per transaction, with a big smile on his face and a bag for the money.

Magaw added, "Normally, you can't take more than $200 at a time, and [most machines] will not allow you on nights and weekends to go beyond a certain limit." He said the man apparently used the card at two banking institutions whose computers didn't "blend together," letting him take huge sums without detection.

Unlike bank tellers, ATMs don't give in to greed, carelessness, or men with stockings over their faces. You can't threaten an ATM, but you can fool it, as the schoolboy armed with a lollipop found out in New Zealand in 1986.

Simon the schoolboy took the cardboard from his lollipop wrapper, put it in an envelope, and stuck it into the ATM deposit slot, punching in a deposit of $1 million in New Zealand currency, amounting to about $650,000 in U.S. currency.

The boy checked his account a few days later to find the money had been credited. He withdrew $10. When the cops didn't appear, he withdrew another $500 but got scared and returned the money.

The next day he withdrew $1,500 but grew frightened again and told one of his instructors at Selwyn College. His headmaster took him to meet with executives at United Building Society savings and loan, the institution he'd hit.

Tony Kunowski, the corporate affairs manager for the savings and loan, said, "We are not amused, but we don't think this is the tip of an iceberg." He said the boy's scheme worked because of the lag in reconciling ATM transactions around the country with the institution's central computer system.

"The delay in toting up the figures would normally be four

weeks and that was how a schoolboy could keep a fake million dollars in his account without anyone batting an eyelid," said Kunowski. "Human error may be involved."

Lollipop larceny's reign of terror is over now that bank officials have caught on to it, but would-be thieves can still take advantage of the weakest link in the system—people. Customers of a Swedish bank in 1986 fell prey to a gang of kids with an imaginative approach to decorating ATMs. They took a stolen badge from a guard company and stuck it with double-sticky tape onto the ATM's money slot. They then disappeared into the shadows and watched someone come up to use the machine. A person making a withdrawal entered his password and the requested amount, but the badge stopped the money from coming out the slot. The machine interpreted this as a disfunction and flashed "technical error" onto the screen. At that point, the disappointed customer left, and the gang took the badge off the slot, removed the money, and replaced the badge for the next victim.

This went on for months, but the bank didn't inform any of its customers, claiming that the publicity would encourage others to cheat. It also didn't refund customers the money stolen unless they complained about the deduction in their bank statements. An uproar of criticism made the bank change its policy and promise to refund stolen money to all customers affected, whether they complained or not.

In a story of dubious veracity, an Italian entrepreneur tried a more sophisticated approach that worked beautifully. Italian ATM clients at one bank were happy to see that their waiting-line problems were solved; the station had another, newly installed terminal. Customers put their cards in the new terminal and answered its request for their secret passwords, but then the machine ate the cards, saying they were invalid and telling customers to visit the bank during working hours and straighten the problem out.

By the time they got to the bank the next day, it was too late. The new "terminal" was actually a personal computer that a hacker had programmed to respond like an ATM. When everyone had left, he retrieved the cards and secret passwords from the terminal and cleaned out the people's accounts.

Some traditionalists reject this kind of slick computer heist, perferring time-honored tools like guns. One story, set in Japan, has all the elements of a James Cagney movie: a kidnapping, a threat, messages planted in the local classifieds, and alert coppers who join forces with the bank to save a little girl.

Someone kidnapped the girl in Tokyo and warned her father that he'd never see his daughter again unless he put the ransom money in his ATM account and printed his account number and password in a certain section of the classifieds. The kidnapper said he would withdraw the money from the account and return the girl. There were hundreds of the bank's ATMs scattered throughout the city, and no one knew what the kidnapper looked like. It sounded like a fail-safe operation.

But when bank programmers heard of the plan, they worked overnight to program the ATMs to trap any transactions for that account and notify bank operators where the withdrawal was taking place. The police department stationed as many officers as it could close to the bank's ATMs in the hope that the kidnapper would show up at one of them.

The father made the deposit, publishing his password and account numbers. The kidnapper chose a deserted ATM on the fringes of the city, put the card in, and pulled out a thick stack of yen notes. But before he could step out of the ATM booth, a policeman grabbed his arm and arrested him. They found the little girl safe and sound. The programmers got a medal. The kidnapper got a jail term.

10

THE MONSTER TURNS...
AND FALLS TO
ITS KNEES

EDINBURGH (Reuters)—A robot dressed in a black hat and bow tie appeared in court on Tuesday after running amok in a restaurant where it was employed to serve wine.

Within its first hour on the job, the secondhand robot became uncontrollable, knocking over furniture, frightening customers and spilling a glass of wine. Eventually its head fell into a customer's lap.

The robot found out what any waitress or waiter knows: serving food is a demanding job, and if you don't keep organized, you can lose your head. Maybe the robot went berserk because it couldn't deal with pressure, but the nation's livelier tabloids are always running stories about computers that attack people out of sheer malice.

One of the articles was on a "demon computer" that struck in Chile. "It's Killed Two Women and Put One in a Coma!" ran the article's subhead. The accompanying graphic was a photo of a desktop terminal, with a horned devil who looked like Gumby gone bad lunging from the screen.

The vice-president of customer relations for a financial firm

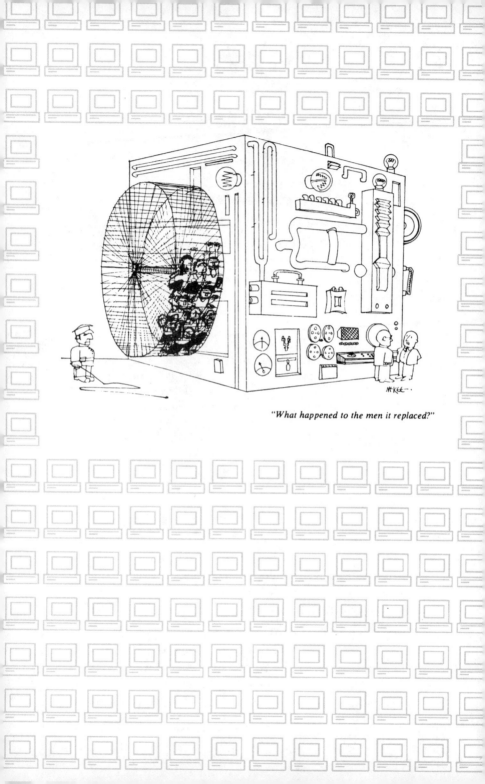

"What happened to the men it replaced?"

in Valparaiso, Chile, said that the bank had installed the computer terminal five months earlier and that it had already zapped three operators, killing two of them. The third was found sitting in front of the screen, mouth open and an empty look in her eyes, in a brain-dead coma. He said the computer shot a burst of electricity out at a workman who tried to remove it, knocking him out. The executive concluded that the bank was recruiting Inca "spiritbreakers" from the Andes to exorcise the machine.

The Russians could use a few good spiritbreakers themselves to deal with a malevolent computer that fried a human chess opponent in March 1989. A tabloid reported that the computer would stand trial for murdering the chess champion Nikolai Gudkov, electrocuted when he touched the metal board he and the machine were playing on, an act a Soviet police investigator called "cold-blooded murder."

The motive? "Niko Gudkov won three straight games and the computer couldn't stand it," said the investigator. "When the chess master reached for his knight to begin play in the fourth game, the computer sent a lethal surge of electricity to the board surface. The computer had been programmed to move its chess pieces by producing a low-level electric current. Gudkov was electrocuted while a gallery of hundreds watched.

"It might sound ridiculous to bring a machine to trial for murder, but a machine that can solve problems and think faster than any human must be held accountable for its actions." One can only hope that this doesn't give the American chess-playing computer Deep Thought any ideas.

The Chaplinesque restaurant robot and the demonic terminals have something in common—their stories act out the science fiction theme of the creation turning on its creator, a theme common in science fiction since the publication of Mary Shelley's *Frankenstein*. In fact, the 1921 play *R.U.R.*, which introduced the word "robot," also portrayed man-made slaves rebelling against their masters. Karel Čapek, the Czechoslovakian writer who wrote the play, invented "robot" from the Czechoslovakian word for "servitude" or "forced labor."

One of the earliest reported robot killings happened in Japan, a country that leads the world in active industrial robots. In 1981, a robot swung out its arm and killed Kendi Urawa at the Kawasaki Heavy Industries robot-building factory in Hyōgo. Investigators surmised that Urawa jumped a fence surrounding a robot instead of opening the gate, which would have automatically shut off the robot's power supply. He apparently wanted to fix another robot, which he thought was malfunctioning, and got pinned by the killer robot's claw.*

Factory robots don't resemble those in pulp fiction. One may consist of a single computer-directed metal arm that performs the same repetitive task, or a delivery cart that rolls along by itself. The sci-fi robot is more in the Frankenstein mode, a cyborg—a robot in human form. From the moment the German movie *Metropolis* unveiled the first gleaming cyborg, it has had a place in fiction as a creation both beautiful and evil. Made more perfect than the most flawless human, it's an avenging angel bent on murder and almost impervious to destruction. It reached its gory glory in *The Terminator,* where Arnold Schwarzenegger played a robot as skilled at massacring humans as at doing home eye surgery. Celluloid cyborgs achieved humanlike complexity in *Blade Runner,* where they flee human control because they desire freedom, murder humans in a rage when they discover they can't escape mortality, seek revenge out of grief, and show a surprising compassion

---

*At the time of Urawa's death, Japan had 75,000 industrial robots, leading the world in programmable robots, followed by the United States, West Germany, France, Sweden, and Britain. The first reported killing of an American at the hands—or rather, the levers—of a robot was in 1984. The die-cast operator Harry Allen of Jackson, Michigan, was pinned by an industrial robot and died five days later at age thirty-four. By the time he died, Japan had had between five and twenty robot-related deaths.

that makes one wonder if they acquired souls somewhere along the assembly line. In *Westworld,* the robots revolt for a more traditional reason; they're tired of being picked on.

Cyborgs are thematically convenient because their human resemblance makes them risk-free scapegoats. When you read a novel in which a bad guy is blown to bloody bits, you may, if the novel's written half well, find your satisfaction dampened by an awareness of that person's humanity, but if a bad cyborg is blown to synthetic bloody bits, it's time to break out the champagne. Portrayals of cyborgs as compassionless thugs without any redeeming value resemble the caricatures of ruthless Huns and bloodthirsty Japs from the two world wars.

Cyborgs are dramatic because of their human image, but your everyday computer, with its everyday power over trash compactors, traffic lights, pacemakers, furnaces, and so on, is less photogenic but potentially more dangerous. Take the computer that controlled a conveyor belt at a cement factory and started lobbing around multi-ton boulders instead of sending them to concrete heaven.

The computer sent boulders up the conveyor to be crushed, after which they were mixed with sand to make cement. A batch of defective computer chips turned off one of the conveyors, which was located some eighty feet above the ground, causing boulders about seven feet in diameter to pile up until they started high-diving over the sides, crushing the cars in the parking lot below. The workers noticed the barrage only after someone heard thuds from the window and looked outside.

Computers during their dinosaur age were enormous, requiring bulky metal parts that could be dangerous if they got out of control. Students at a dorm party years ago recalled the Metal Razor Spaghetti Horror in a group conversation that shows how a story's shape changes when a number of people tell it. The students are herein christened the Teller, the Doubter, the Elaborator, and the Sequeler:

Teller: In the old days they used to have big, heavy metal tapes instead of what they use now. One time the machine wasn't taking the tape up right, and it started flying out of the tape drive at high speed, chasing the programmers around the room.

Elaborator: The big old Bryant disks. The story I heard was that once one got loose, cut through a wall, sliced two cars in half across the street.

Doubter: Then cut down every tree in the forest.

Sequeler: A manufacturer started putting metallic decorations on its tapes to make them pretty, and they apparently had to stop doing that because the computer would spin the tapes around and the overhead fluorescent lights would flash on them and make this dazzling pattern that hypnotized operators.

The students also told stories about card feeders that hunger for human flesh. One waited like a Venus flytrap until an unsuspecting night operator got too close. It grabbed his arm and pulled him in, trapping the night operator in a half-crouch that was both undignified and exhausting. He couldn't reach the telephone, and no one else was around, so he was imprisoned there until the morning operator stepped in.

A similar story featured an IBM repairman whose regulation tie almost earned him a promotion to that big blue corporation in the sky. He was bending over the card feeder when it snatched his tie and yanked him in up to his chin. Fortunately, someone passing by the room heard him gasping, "Stop this damn thing," and, after only a few seconds' thought, decided to free him.

If the MIT students who told this story can be believed, the computers really had it in for one computer science professor, who seemed to incite robots to homicide. Once, someone demonstrating a computer-operated arm unwisely left the machine to the mercies of restless hackers. They wrote programs that made it pick up blocks and hurl them across the room at the professor, who happened to be passing by. In another tale, the same guy was at the MIT Artificial Intelligence Laboratory when a robot arm rushed him and cornered him. Recognizing the futility of having tenure if you're about to be smashed to pulp, he cried for help and a hacker ran to his aid, typing in a program that stopped the robot in the nick of time. It's a hacker's closet Superman dream: the trapped mentor about to get fatally dinged by a robot is rescued by a savior flying forth on winged Florsheims.

The author Steven Levy describes a near-tragedy in which the MIT Artificial Intelligence Laboratory director Marvin Minsky almost became the world's first Ping-Pong fatality:

> The hackers actually did get the robot to hold a paddle and take a good swat at a ball lobbed in its direction. Bill Bennett would later recall a time when Minsky stepped into the robot arm's area, floodlit by the bright lights required by the vidicon camera; the robot, seeing the glare reflecting from Minsky's bald dome, mistook the professor for a large Ping-Pong ball and nearly decapitated him.

MIT students give the artificial intelligence researcher Ed Fredkin credit for inventing the much imitated (at least in legend) walking disk drives. According to the story, when Fredkin and friends were working for the Army, they designed programs that made IBM tape drives stop suddenly after reaching top speed, causing them to jerk around so much that the drives would rock back and forth and finally fall over. After a few runs this would destroy the drive, but then, what price art? Eventually the group received a nasty letter from Army brass telling them to knock it off.

If Fredkin did originate this trick, he started a craze. Go to any major computer department, and someone will have a walking-computer story in which his adviser or roommate or best friend or Aunt Beattie got the disk drives to stroll across a room, sending terror into the hearts of the populace. The disk drives are said to be made to walk when the operator runs programs that cause them to rotate back and forth 180 degrees in rapid succession, until harmonic motion builds up to such a pitch that the drives and all that's attached to them break free of their cases and stagger like Boris Karloff onto the floor.

Another chunk of hardware that inspired respect in the early days was the computer's mammoth memory drum, about the size of the cylinder on a steamroller. A Georgia Tech instructor remembered the following:

> I used to have a whole bunch of fast Rand drums, which are about as long as a classroom table but a good bit deeper. I love fast Rand drums. The drums are iron-oxide-coated, solid steel cylinders with enormous amounts of rotational energy stored up inside. Drums beat hell out of disks; they're much faster, there's so much energy tied up in them.
>
> An operator told me that one time a drum got loose in a shop that had 36040s and UNIVAC 1108s. It just came off its spindles and steamrolled out of its cabinet through a concrete block wall. This was on night shift, the graveyard shift.
>
> The shop operator sat at his console with its blinking lights and a little shelf-like desk on it for setting his sandwich and his coffee and his boots. So here he is leaning back in his chair with his feet up on the console, and this runaway Rand went right through the CP under his feet, just flattened it, then wedged itself into a bank of power supplies.

Computer experts who dismiss such tales as myth will talk in their next breath about the computer company that tried to show how tough its machine was by pulling it out of its air-conditioned cloister and setting it up in the back of a semitrailer. It worked fine until the truck turned a corner and the memory drum's inertia took charge, flipping the vehicle over. In another version, a U.S. Navy ship whose computers have memory drums turns just as the operators spin the horizontal drums up to speed. The drums become huge gyroscopes, ripping free of their restraints and barreling through the ship.

For better or for worse, huge memory drums are obsolete. The military no longer outfits computers with memory drums—it gives them guns, instead. If computer-generated firing mishaps have caused fatalities, the military's been unsurprisingly quiet about them. A few near-misses have made news, however. In August 1983, the U.S. Navy admitted that an errant computer forced a warship's three-inch gun to fire in the opposite direction from its target during naval exercises off of San Francisco. The frigate *George Philip* of the Pacific Fleet Surface Forces fired a three-inch shell that landed either nine miles from a Mexican merchant ship or—depending on who's telling the story—just one mile off. The *Los Angeles Times* reported that a computerized radar-directed gun used on tanks, called the Sergeant York, declined to focus on practice targets of low-flying planes during military exercises. Instead, it kept turning toward large buildings, identifying them as targets.

A possible computer malfunction on an armed Air Force jet in 1989 almost blew up Marion County, Georgia. An F-16 jet from Moody Air Force Base accidentally released a live bomb during a training flight over Fort Benning's "Kilo Impact Area." The pilot tried to release the bomb over the practice range, but it wouldn't drop, and as he circled back over Marion County, it fell. Ninety kilograms of explosives blew up in a wooded area, shaking the windows of houses almost half a mile away.

Electromagnetic radiation from military transmitters might have made the bomb drop by detonating the electro-explosive devices that release it. Electromagnetic interference has also

caused problems with the Army's UH-60 "Black Hawk" heli-
copter, which has been banned from flying near certain transmitters worldwide as a result. The Air Force is examining
whether pulsed radar beams from military stations can trigger
the release devices in both military and commercial planes.

Equally dangerous and more insidious are malfunctions in
industrial software or microchips, such as those that control
fuel rods in nuclear power plants. We depend so much on
computers that we tend to be blind to their presence until
something goes wrong. In one joke about suspect software, passengers on a Boeing 747 about to fly to England are settling
into their seats when a bodiless, synthesized voice speaks on the
intercom:

> Good morning, ladies and gentlemen of flight 117. I am
> the captain for your flight, a TXX 1223 designed by AA
> Licknaprayer Aerospace Industries. I am the latest in super-
> computer design, with a quadruple redundancy backup sys-
> tem to assure optimum performance. So please, sit back and
> relax during your flight. The flight attendants will soon be
> serving complimentary beverages, and today's movie is free
> in honor of this historic occasion. Let me assure you that this
> autopilot system is superior to human control, and that
> everything is perfectly safe . . . perfectly safe . . . perfectly
> safe . . .

A computer programmer hit the European lecture circuit in
the 1970s and used the airplane story to warn people about the
importance of well-designed software. He'd give this example:
"Say you're on an airplane and a voice comes on saying there
are no pilots aboard, the entire flight will be run by computer,
and the program was designed by one of your students. Would
you stay on that plane?"

That usually made his point as the audience nodded in agreement. However, during one talk he noticed that a man sitting in the front row didn't nod, but just leaned back and smiled. After the talk he approached the man, who turned out to be a French computer science professor, and said, "I couldn't help but notice that you seemed quite calm. Would you stay on the plane?"

"But of course," the man replied.

"You must have exceptionally fine students," the lecturer said.

"No, you misunderstand me," the professor replied. "You see, if it was one of my graduate students, the plane wouldn't take off at all!"

His comment reveals the major chink in the mechanical Goliath's armor—humans who, unwittingly or not, sling pebbles at the giant's brain that bring it crashing to its knees. The pebbles can be as accidental as a single error in a program or as deliberate as glue in the disk drive. For instance, MIT hackers used to crash the Multics computer many moons ago by sending all the elevators to the top floor simultaneously. The system would interpret the resulting power surge as a power failure and would crash.

Some hackers delight in discovering and exploiting the computer's vulnerabilities. They were probably the same kids who kept crashing their model airplanes and blowing up their home chemistry sets, always insisting it was an accident.

Thomas J. Padula of Princeton University heard a story about a Caltech student who bragged to IBM that he could program an IBM PC-XT, a personal computer, to destroy itself. IBM executives replied that if he could do that in front of witnesses, they'd give him a free new PC.

The day of reckoning came, and so did IBM. The representatives gave the student a PC-XT and sat down to watch. He turned the computer on, inserted a disk, and leaned back. Soon the machine started violently shaking, then came sounds of crackling circuitry, smoke poured out, and the power supply shut down. He'd destroyed the machine.

His software Shiva had ordered the computer's disk drive to swing back and forth at a frequency that made the machine case shake back and forth as well. The more the disk drive shook, the more it increased the case's shaking, causing massive vibrations inside that made the mother board flex until it crashed and sent live electrical parts snapping into each other, triggering short circuits, small explosions, and wild sparks that demolished the power supply.

Another programming sleight of hand didn't ignite pyro-technics but did cause widespread panic when it simultaneously paralyzed computers across the United States. The catastrophe started at Brookhaven National Laboratory, in Upton, New York, when a mainframe suddenly died and couldn't be revived. The laboratory staff called the nearby Grumman Corporation because it had an identical computer, only to hear that Grumman's computer had also just broken down for no apparent reason. So the laboratory people called the manufacturer, but before they could complain they received the frantic reply, "We can't talk to you now. Everything's gone crazy. Every one of our computers in the country seems to have come down with an error."

The ghost in the machine was a forgotten function that could automatically turn off the mainframe on a given date. It turned out no one really needed a feature like that, and that it could even mess up computer operations if it were used, so the computer company's chief programmer decided to cancel out the function by feeding a large number into it. Unfortunately, computers fed that number read it as a date twelve years in the future, so when the computers' clocks reached that date, the forgotten function told the machines to turn themselves off, and every machine in the country went dead.

Though it may look imposing, the computer is surprisingly fragile, resembling less a Goliath than that scrawny kid in fifth grade with smudged glasses and numerous allergies who was always sneezing.

In fact, computers are subject to hay fever, or at least their chips are, as a California computer chip manufacturer learned. The factory's high yields of quality chips plummeted every Thursday. Management quietly monitored employees who worked in the "clean room" where the chips were made. Did some party hearty on Wednesday night and return hung over and careless on Thursday? Was someone with a grudge sabotaging chips? The villain turned out to be the company landscaper, who mowed the lawn every Thursday, sending clouds of pollen into the air. People entering the building carried pollen in with them on their clothing, contaminating hundreds of thousands of chips, which is nothing to sneeze at.

Subtler and far deadlier than pollen was the attack of the devouring fungus, which struck New England. A major computer company had serious problems with one of its clients, a utility company that stored data on enormous magnetic tapes. The tapes were inexplicably losing information; a tape would work fine one day, miss some data the next, and be totally blank the next. The utility had millions of customer files on the tapes, and even backup tapes were losing data to the plague.

The computer company sent flocks of repairmen out to dissect the system and examine it. It looked fine. Next, they shipped the defective tapes to Boulder, Colorado, for specialists to test. The Boulder staff found a strange oxidation on the reels. They replaced the tapes and sent them back, and everything hummed along just fine—for ninety days. Then the tapes self-destructed again. The strange oxidation was reborn.

The engineers were almost resigned to the fact that they would lose irreplaceable data, but then a clever field engineer examined the computer's read-write heads, which read tapes and remove dust particles from them. She discovered that the heads were covered with the same oxidation. Could the read-write heads be transmitting something from tape to tape?

She investigated the history of the old tapes and found that they'd been stored in a large repository carved inside a mountain, a cavern made to withstand nuclear attack. The storage area was dry and secure, but overcrowded, so the utility was storing tapes in an adjoining room where a mycologist was experimenting with strains of fungi. One fungus had attacked the tapes, hitched a ride on them to data central, and transmitted itself onto the read-write heads. Because the utility sent tapes to banks and other businesses as part of its billing, the devouring fungus—which really *was* a fungus—had spread throughout the Boston area. Utility representatives spent months quietly visiting local businesses, warning them of their lurking intruder and replacing tapes for free.

Mother Nature has an arsenal of ways besides fungus to subdue computers. When a Chicago bank installed a computer system many years ago, something fishy acted up. The computers kept overheating and shutting down. Engineers traced the problem to the computer's cooling system, which relied on water piped out of Lake Michigan. Schools of fish were clogging the cooling system's intake valves and choking it off. What kind of kamikaze fish attacked the computer is not said, but if you've ever staggered along the shores of Lake Michigan during alewife season, you can guess the culprit. Squirrels and racoons have also been known to sacrifice their lives in late-night commando raids against computers, frying themselves by crawling into transformers or power stations and shorting the circuits.

Even the sun unleashed its wrath in a story set in Los Angeles during the late 1960s at a company that had just installed a new computer room on the tenth floor of a downtown high rise, one of the tallest buildings in the city at the time, with walls of sleek glass. Its computer was running about thirty tapes overnight, since it was behind schedule. As soon as rosy-fingered dawn snapped up the night shades in the sky, all the tapes went into high-speed rewind and sent ribbons billowing out over the floor.

It turned out that when sunlight shone on the tapes, it struck their end-of-tape sensors, causing them to rewind. Like vampires, the computer tapes were helpless in sunlight, so the night-shift supervisor got the new duty of making sure the drapes were closed before the sun came up.

Another legendary debacle triggered by light hit at a highly publicized affair thrown by IBM, ironic considering that IBM is the master of the seamless image. D. E. Rosenheim, who helped develop the IBM 701, the first mass-produced modern commercial computer, recalled the famous faux pas, which occurred when the company held a dedication ceremony for the 701's installation at its New York headquarters. Top-level executives, the engineering team, and a gang of reporters crowded the ceremony room.

"Things went pretty well at the dedication," said Rosenheim, "until the photographers started taking pictures of the hardware. As soon as the flash bulbs went off, the whole system came down. Following a few tense moments on the part of the engineering crew, we realized with some consternation that the light from the flash bulbs was erasing the information in the CRT memory. Suffice it to say that shortly thereafter the doors to the CRT storage frame were made opaque to the offending wavelengths."

Those ignorant of how delicate a computer is can accidentally damage it more than can someone who deliberately plans its ruin. In one incident, the only clue after each crash of a cluster of mainframes was a small pile of sawdust, materializing whenever the mainframes crashed. Stakeouts didn't turn up any culprits.

One day, a programmer lounging by a mainframe saw a maintenance man stroll in with a two-by-four. He jammed the wood between two mainframes that happened to be just far enough apart to hold the wood in place, then sawed it in half, gathered the pieces, and walked out. He left behind a pile of sawdust and a system that crashed by the vibrations from his power saw.

The physics department at the University of California at Berkeley was the site for another ghostly glitch. Late at night, experimentalists taking sensitive computer readings on continuous graph paper would see the recording pen go haywire, as if an earthquake were rattling the campus, though it was a bizarre earthquake, appearing at the same time each night and lasting for the same period. They traced it to the night custodian, who polished the linoleum on the ground floor during those hours. Vibrations from his floor polisher rattled the equipment two floors above.

Another maintenance person turned a computer room into something resembling a frantic Los Vegas casino, as a Georgia Tech computer instructor recalled:

> She was a new operator on a computer system at the state crime and toxicology lab, a big, tall, brown-haired gal, real handsome thing, but she was a little scatter-brained. . . . It was a twenty-four-hour operation that had a laundromat of disk drives—two rows of them, just like walking into a laundromat of washing machines, nine-platter mothers spinning up a storm.
>
> She was on watch one evening, and one of her duties was to clean the read-write heads on the disk drives—a read-write head is a little disk of porcelain on a metal wand. She opened a can of alcohol and went down the aisle cleaning the heads, brushing, brushing, brushing, nine platters with about sixteen heads on each one. Half an hour later the whole damn room turned into a craps parlor.
>
> What she had done was she had grabbed of bottle of

acetone instead of alcohol, and it softened the epoxy that attached the ceramic to the steel! The heads would rattle loose and start popping off, whacking the 360-revolutions-per-minute platter and shooting all over the room, going "ping ping POW."

A wedding ring launched a crash in Houston, Texas. To everyone's puzzlement, the mainframe went down every morning at six o'clock. The manager walked in early one day, anticipating a crash, and saw an operator listening to the six o'clock radio show. As the show's theme song began, the operator unconsciously strummed his fingers in rhythm to the song on top of the central processing unit, tapping it with his wedding ring. Within seconds, the machine went down.

The manager had the system brought up again and asked the operator for a repeat performance. The machine crashed again after ten taps. They decided that something was shaken out of place by the tapping, and solved the problem by asking the operator to restrict his musical appreciation to humming.

A strange miasma kept downing a computer at Caltech during the late 1970s. Its disk would head crash several times during the year, grinding into the magnetic coatings and stripping off large disk slivers, demolishing the drive. Repairmen kept replacing the disk drive, which kept committing hara-kiri, and they grew increasingly irritated that the disk should smash itself up in a clean, well-maintained computer room.

One day, a repairman realized that the copy machine sitting in the hall outside the computer was driving the disk to suicide. The copy machine toner evaporated and leaked. Being denser than air, the fumes drifted to the floor and got sucked under the computer room door because of the room's negatively pressurized ventilation. Once inside, they slowly delaminated the disk until it exploded.

Given the right circumstances, even a child can bring the

monster to its knees. Take the case of the industrialist who came home from work one day and turned on her home computer. She pulled out the master disk and tried to push it into the disk drive, but nothing happened. Instead of sliding in, the disk just squished.

She put it down and peered into the slot to see something orange glowing inside. She turned off the machine, fetched some tweezers, and fished out the culprit. It turned out that her three-year-old daughter wanted to work on the computer just like Mommy did, but, not having her own software, she tried to program it with a square of sliced cheese.

The monster can turn on its creator, or it can be brought to its knees by the most innocent human, or there is a third scenario: those controlling the computer grow careless and unleash its power dangerously. A grisly incident happened when a neurologist conducting experiments on a monkey with electrodes planted in its brain called repairmen to examine the computer that recorded the monkey's brain waves.

The repairmen weren't used to working with computers linked to lab animals, so they weren't in the habit of considering what might happen if they disrupted a machine whose electrodes ran into a living brain. They failed to disconnect the monkey from the computer while running diagnostic tests, which did peculiar things to the monkey's brain, killing it. Since then, biologists with a macabre sense of humor advise researchers testing lab computers to use a "scratch monkey" first, a lab animal equivalent to a "scratch disk," something you put into the computer during testing and can sacrifice without much problem if things go wrong.

In the world outside the laboratory, the "scratch monkey" can be a human at the mercy of computer experts so caught up with the machine's beauty that they forget whom it is supposed to serve. Since humans are more pliable than computers, it can be easier to make a human fit the computer's limitations than to design the computer to fit the human's needs. When that happens, the human becomes a prisoner trapped by the computer rather than liberated by it, which may not kill the "scratch monkey" but can make him miserable. This reversal of priorities worries some computer experts, who see in it a danger as potentially oppressive as a computerized police state. A typical example of this was a controversy over airline pilots flying late schedules who kept falling asleep at their computerized controls, bringing suggestions that computers be programmed to blast the pilots with loud sounds to keep them awake.

"Let them sleep!" commented Don Norman of the University of California at San Diego. "Human physiology and psychology are reasonably fixed. . . . Too many of our technologies are designed with only the technology in mind, and the human is forced to cope. Then when the problems occur, we blame either the technology itself or the person. But neither is to blame—it is the design and use of the technology that is wrong. . . . Creativity, adaptability, flexibility, and extreme reliability are our strengths. Continual alertness and precision in action or memory are our weaknesses. Why not use technology in ways that take advantage of the former and allow for the latter?"

When human habit is ignored in the computerized designing of our world, people might feel they have no control over their lives, becoming passive and demoralized. Or, they might react violently, as in India in 1986 when New Delhi transportation workers imposed a computerized bus route system they called "enlightened traffic management." The designers ignored the citizens' deeply entrenched travel habits.

The public didn't dance in the streets when the new routes took effect; instead, it rioted. Former bus passengers communicated their displeasure by shattering transportation department windows and deflating bus tires. Crowds stormed the streets in protest marches, complaining the new routes didn't take them where they wanted to go. The riots lasted four days.

On the fifth day, the New Delhi Transport Corporation caved in and scrapped the "rationalized" routes in favor of the former ones. As transportation workers drove down the streets, announcing through loudspeakers that they were restoring the old routes, thousands of triumphant commuters followed them, shouting, "The computer has failed!"

But it wasn't the computer that failed—it was those who programmed it. They forgot the paradox of power the computer brings; if human needs don't remain supreme, the computer's masters will wind up its slaves.

GLOSSARY

AMYL FAX SHUFFLE TIME. A time-delay program meant as a joke in which the perpetrator invents a message, adds its target's name, and sends it. The message boomerangs right back, looking for all the world as if the target sent it and causing great hilarity when the perpetrator confronts the target about the (often insulting) message, leaving the innocent target to squirm in confusion. Guess you have to be there to appreciate it.

ANDROID. A robot built to resemble a person.

ARTIFICIAL REALITY SYSTEM. A computer system in which a person using a mask, gloves, and perhaps a bodysuit, all linked to a computer, is plunged into the computer's synthesized "world," with its own illusions of space, time, and matter.

BABBAGE DISEASE. Named after the nineteenth-century mathematician and eccentric Charles Babbage, arguably the inventor of the first modern computer and the first person to suffer from a computer-related malady. Babbage disease is the obsession to perfect hardware or software, blacking out practical concerns such as getting a job done or getting a job, period. Symptoms: almost all waking hours spent with computers; constant talk about computers; a habit of sleeping in computer rooms; indifference to circadian rhythms or members of the opposite sex; repulsive personal hygiene. Babbage disease sufferers tape broken glasses frames with Band-Aids. Cure: there is no cure, but the condition can be treated. The most successful treatment is to drug the victim and bundle him off to a remote Australian outback where no one has heard the word "megabyte." The least successful cure is to tell the victim that there's more to life than computers. The victim will just respond with a blank expression and the question "What?"

BACK DOOR. A secret password that programmers conceal in a system so that they can enter the system even if their regular passwords have been revoked.

BAGBITER. Equipment or program that fails, usually intermittently. Usage verges on obscenity, as in "This bagbiting system won't let me sign off." (From the 1988 Jargon file kept on netwire at Stanford and MIT.)

BANANA. A sweet, yellowish, oblong tropical fruit, high in potassium, that should never be fed into a computer's card reader.

BIT BUCKET. An invisible pail into which missing data falls. Diginerds carry bit buckets to hold stolen data.

BLETCH. From German *brechen,* "to vomit." A term of disgust.

BLETCHER. An outsider to computer culture.

BLETCHEROUS. Disgusting in design or function. Usage is slightly comic. (From the 1988 Jargon file kept on netwire at Stanford and MIT.)

BUG. An often elusive problem in hardware or software. The term is at least a century old and probably originated in electrical engineering.

COBOL CHARLIE. A denigratory term for someone who knows how to use the COBOL computer language but doesn't know how it works.

COMPUSPEAK. The specialized technical jargon of computer aficionados.

COMPUTERITE. Synonyms: computer fan, computer expert or professional, hacker, "compulsive programmer" (Weizenbaum); in general, someone knowledgeable about computers, but each synonym has different shades of meaning. A computer expert is anyone who knows a lot about the machine. A compulsive programmer is someone who has an emotional attachment to computers stronger than that between a boy and his dog. See also BABBAGE DISEASE and HACKERTUDE.

COMPUTER KOAN. A pithy, mystical, and instructive parable about computers.

CORE DUMP. When a computer's main memory pulls itself out of its regular operating mode, causing a memory fault, it is said to "core dump." Core dumps usually happen when a software bug triggers unsavory events.

CRASH. (1) To run into something with great force. (2) To be in a motor vehicle that is engaging in a mishap. (3) To go to sleep. (4) To have a bad reaction to mind-altering drugs. (5) (Possible future definition) to be mentally overwhelmed and collapsing from an information overload.

CUSPY. Exciting, beautiful, interesting. Often said of a particularly good program, and rarely said about sex, whose excitement pales beside that of a truly cuspy program. How do hard-core hackers reproduce, anyway? Viruses?

CYBERNETICS. The art of creating computers that mimic human abilities, and of studying control systems in biological, mechanical, and electronic systems. The computer pioneer Norbert Wiener coined the word from the Greek word for "steersman," *kybernetes.*

CYBERPUNK. High-tech version of the 1950s hood who is into computers rather than cars. This cause without a rebel cruises AT&T networks instead of Main Street and breaks into Pentagon computers rather than condom machines. (By Thomas J. Cook of the North Texas PC Users Group.)

CYBORG. A robot built to resemble a person in a very bad mood. "Cyborg" is commonly used in science fiction stories, perhaps because it sounds nastier than "android." Androids might be sly and malevolent, but they look like your favorite high school teacher so you feel tempted to trust them. Cyborgs are rarely considerate; they prefer ripping the heads off of space explorers rather than politely asking them to pass the sugar.

DIGINERDS. Invisible sprites that jump inside a computer, causing it to fail. Synonym; "gremlins."

DISGUSTITUDE. A typical example of how computerites hack the English language to bits and reassemble it to their own evil ends. "Disgustitude" means a state of disgust.

DWIM! "Do What I Mean!" A command a programmer shouts to his computer when it fails to do what he wants it to do, and does only what he programmed it to do. It's a request that the computer read his mind.

ELEGANT. In mathematics, physics, and computer science, "elegant" describes an equation or program that is simple yet profound.

FLAME. To drone on and on about a boring topic, such as anything not involving computers.

FOOBAR. Also known as FUBAR, this is an acronym for Fouled Up (or Fucked Up) Beyond All Recognition. The term originated in the military sometime around World War II but has been appropriated in computer slang. (1) A mild expression of annoyance over a balky program. (2) A program that's fouled up beyond all recognition. (3) The combination of two hypothetical functions, the FOO and the BAR function, that together create a new function.

GENIUS. An easily guessed password used by idiots.

ʌʌʌ. Used during netwire conversations to signify giggling. (From the 1988 Jargon file kept on netwires at Stanford and MIT.)

GIGO. "Garbage In, Garbage Out," meaning that a computer's output is only as good as its input.

GLASS COCKPIT SYNDROME. A psychology term describing a person stressed by coping with an avalanche of data. It stems from modern commercial and fighter jets whose cockpits are crammed with sensors, trackers, and data outputs. Quick reflexes and a keen eye are secondary; today's fighter jock must be skilled at sorting data from the dozens of streams of information being constantly fed him. He must, in effect, be a human information processor.

GLORK. A mildly unpleasant surprise.

GROK. To understand profoundly, usually in a global sense. (From the 1988 Jargon file kept on netwires at Stanford and MIT.) The word itself is from the science fiction writer Robert Heinlein's novel *Stranger in a Strange Land*.

GUN. To terminate a computer program or job with extreme prejudice, often with malicious intent.

GWEEP. An overworked hacker.

HACK. A verb meaning to tool around with a computer, usually for fun, but sometimes for mischief.

HACKER. (1) Someone knowledgeable about computers. (2) Someone who spends as much time as possible playing with computers. (3) Someone who delights in refining programs, breaking into "secure" systems, reading classified computer files, and watching reruns of "War Games." (4) Someone who breaks into other people's systems and vandalizes them for fun or extortion. This last definition is the most recent one and appears to be gaining preeminence, making "hacker" a dirty word. Hackers themselves have a different word for computer fiends who break into systems and cause mischief. They call such knaves "crackers."

HACKERTUDE. The state of being enthralled by the machine. Unlike Babbage disease, it has no specific symptoms and is not as severe. Someone with Babbage disease doesn't recognize that there's a world beyond computers; someone in hackertude does, but doesn't care. However, a person in the late stages of hackertude comes to resent the machine's dominance in his life and eventually breaks free of the obsession.

HACKIFICATION. (1) The process of turning into a hacker. (2) The act of hacking around with a computer.

HEAD CRASH. What occurs when a computer's read-write head touches a disk's surface, which can cause permanent damage.

IHI! A form of greeting, possibly obsolete, used by FORTRAN programmers to indicate both "hello" and that their meeting turns a new page in their relationship. IHI is a FORTRAN command that tells the computer to start a new page.

INFINITE LOOP. The condition in which a computer endlessly repeats a series of steps, usually because of a programming flaw. Deven E. Ben-Hur of Toronto gave these examples of infinite loops:

One of my favorite ways of defining an infinite loop in a language similar to Modula-2 is:

```
const HellFreezesOver = false;

REPEAT
    stuff
UNTIL HellFreezesOver;
```

Here's a variant:

```
# define Death 1
# define Taxes 1
while (Death && Taxes) (stuff)
```

INFINITELY FINE!   Great beyond belief. Awesome. The cat's pajamas. A consummation devoutly to be wished. Wondrous strange.

KAFKA.   An Austrian novelist and short story writer whose tales about ponderous bureaucracies run by passionate madmen for absurd reasons anticipated the computer industry.

KLUDGE.   (1) A crude solution to fixing a bug or problem. (2) An overly elaborate, awkwardly constructed setup, such as the intricate mousetraps in Rube Goldberg or Heath Robinson cartoons. "Heath Robinson," by the way, was the name of one of ULTRA's top-secret code-cracking electromechanical computers in World War II.

LIVEWARE.   Also called humans, or, more frequently, graduate students. The liveware's expertise, when harnessed by computer-illiterate professors, allows those professors to operate computers they don't understand in order to generate more research grants. (Word coined by Ron Fox, physics department, Georgia Tech.)

MYTHICAL MAN-MONTH.   The observation by the software engineer Fred P. Brooks, Jr., that a job time estimate cannot be done simply by multiplying the number of hours a job requires by the number of people required to carry it out. Brooks noted that people and time are interchangeable units only when there's no communication among individuals. Since communicating is the life's blood of computers, that factor can't be ignored. Adding people to a project can actually *lengthen* the time needed to do the project because time will be spent explaining the project to newcomers, telling them where the bathroom is, taking them out for long lunches to get acquainted, flirting, and so on.

NERD.   Someone who has mastered a technical discipline and sincerely believes that the precision of technology is more appealing than the uncertainty of social culture. (Defined by the *Personal Computing* columnist Paul Saffo.) The word originated in a book by Dr. Seuss, *If I Ran the Zoo.*

OPTICAL COMPUTER.   A type of computer, still largely experimental, that uses laser beams instead of wires to process information and works far faster than traditionally wired computers.

PHONE PHREAKS. Hackers who enjoy messing around with telecommunications systems, often illegally.

POTTY EFFECT. (1) The added thrust of jettisoned human waste on a space vehicle's velocity. (2) Unanticipated effects of human activity in man-machine undertakings.

RAVE. (1) To babble on authoritatively about a subject one knows little about. (2) To whine about a problem to someone who is not in a position to remedy it. (3) To insist on discussing something no one else wants to talk about. (From the 1988 Jargon file kept on netwires at Stanford and MIT.)

ROBOT. A machine, usually computerized, that mimics human actions. The word originated from a Czechoslovakian term for "labor" or "forced servitude."

SCRATCH MONKEY. A macabre term used in biological research to refer to an expendable lab animal that can be wired to lab computers during test runs or when the computer's acting unpredictably.

SOFTWARE DARWINISM. The belief that all software should be free for everyone's use while its creators make a living through other means or else just wither away. Software Darwinism is a survival-of-the-fittest philosophy with altruistic overtones. It would benefit users whose love of software outstrips their wallets, and forsake software designers who lack the talents of other designers able to get decent consulting work but who still like computers and want to be able to design software full-time.

SPORTDEATH. Going on marathon computer sessions without sleep or decent food until the body is on the verge of collapse. Those courting sportdeath play Dungeons and Dragons for thirty hours straight, subsisting on flat soda, potato chips, greasy pizza, and other forms of aortic cement, and flog their bodies to masochistic lengths so that their minds can experience the euphoria of total computer absorption.

STRUCTURED DESIGN. Program development technique which stresses the stepwise decomposition of problems in an egoless environment. Often results in the spontaneous decomposition of egos. (Definition by Thomas J. Cook of the North Texas PC Users Group.)

Spiritbreakers. Indian holy women and men from the Andes occasionally called upon to exorcise demon computers.

Technodolts. (1) Jerks who know only enough about computers to get themselves and others into trouble. (2) Persons who don't understand electrical technology in almost any form, and as a result send tape spinning onto the floor when they program their VCR or shoot out sprays of hot water when they try to use an automatic coffee maker. Dangerous persons to be near.

Technodweebs. (1) A self-derogatory term for people heavily interested in technology. (2) A derisive term for neophytes who think they understand technology and become insufferable as a result.

Technoterrorists. People who maliciously hack into other people's systems to destroy or cripple files, often as a form of extortion or revenge. Also called technopaths.

Technotwits. People who believe they know a lot about computers.

Technoweenies. People who are more socially maladapted than nerds, if that's possible, and have trouble dealing with other people outside of a technological environment. (Definition by Russ Kepler of Albuquerque, New Mexico.)

Tense. A clever and efficient program. A tense programmer is one who produces tense code. (From the 1988 Jargon file kept on netwires at Stanford and MIT.) Possible origin: an amalgam of "dense" (as in "compact") and of "terse."

Thrashing. Having so much to do that one becomes disoriented and disorganized, now starting one project, dropping that to begin another, leaving that to try something else, until one ends up helplessly watching the breakfast eggs fry into brown, lacey lumps because flipping them with a spatula seems like such a complicated procedure. Thrashing is a gweep's usual condition.

Thule incident. A 1960 NORAD computer error that almost triggered a nuclear war.

Top-down design. Program design methodology equivalent to solving a maze by starting at the treasure chest in the middle (the program goal) and tracing backward to see how to get there. Works flawlessly if you do indeed start at the program goals. A decidedly dull approach to programming. (Definition by Thomas J. Cook of the North Texas PC Users Group.)

VANILLA. Something boring, like a boring program.

VAPORWARE. A form of software similar to Santa Claus and the Easter Bunny.

VIRUS. The computer culture's version of the joy buzzer. A virus is a program that duplicates itself once it gets into a system and inserts itself into other programs, often causing trouble. A "worm" is similar to a virus except that it causes trouble by duplicating itself uncontrollably until it clogs the system and brings it to a standstill.

YOYO MODE. The condition of a system that keeps crashing and coming up again. (From the 1988 Jargon file kept on netwires at Stanford and MIT.)

INDEX